D1521986

Springer Series on Social Work
Albert R. Roberts, D.S.W., Series Editor

Graduate School of Social Work, Rutgers, The State University of New Jersey
Advisory Board: Gloria Bonilla-Santiago, Ph.D., Miriam Dinerman, D.S.W., Sheldon R. Gelman, Ph.D., Gilbert J. Greene, Ph.D., Jesse Harris, D.S.W., Michael J. Smith, D.S.W., and Julia Watkins, Ph.D.

Managing Work and Family Life

Viola M. Lechner, DSW
Michael A. Creedon, DSW

Springer Publishing Company
New York

Springer Publishing Company, Inc.
536 Broadway
New York, NY 10012-3955

94 95 96 97 98 / 5 4 3 2 1

Library of Congress Cataloging-in-Publication Data

Lechner, Viola.
   Managing work and family life / Viola Lechner,
Michael Creedon.
     p. cm. — (Springer series on social work)
   Includes bibliographical references and index.
   ISBN 0-8261-8470-7
   1. Work and family—United States. I. Creedon, Michael A., 1941– .
II. Title. III. Series
HD4904.25.L43 1994
306.3'6'0973—dc20   94–15849
                                             CIP

Printed in the United States of America

To my husband, Sanford Lechner, and my grown children, Debbie McDowell and Diana Pirie for their love, support, and good humor throughout my work life.

(V.M.L.)

To my parents, John and Gretta Creedon, who successfully ran several businesses while raising a large family. They provided an inspiring model of work-family integration.

(M.A.C.)

Viola M. Lechner, DSW, Assistant Professor at St. John's University, holds a doctorate of social welfare from Columbia University. Her dissertation was a study of employees who cared for elderly parents. She has published numerous articles related to work and family issues, as well as having given several presentations to national associations on this topic. She is actively involved in the Committee on Work and Family Issues of the National Association of Social Workers. She is a member of the Eldercare Task Force of the New York Business Group on Health.

Michael A. Creedon, DSW, a graduate of All Hallows College, Dublin, holds a masters degree in social work from Virginia Commonwealth University, and a doctorate in social welfare from the University of Maryland. He is President of The Creedon Group, international consultants on aging issues, and Visiting Professor of Gerontology and Social Work at University College, Cork in Ireland. He is a member of the part-time faculty in the College of Continuing Studies at Johns Hopkins University. Dr. Creedon is a consultant to The Office of Family Policy at the U.S. Department of Defense, the National Conference of State Legislatures, the Health Research Board of Ireland, Carlow International, Public Service Electric and Gas Company of New Jersey, and other organizations. He has published widely on aging issues. He was senior author of the first resource book on eldercare for corporate employees, *The Pepsico Eldercare Resource Guide* (1986), editor of *Issues for An Aging America: Employees and Eldercare* (1987), senior author of *Eldercare in the Workplace* (1989), and co-author of *Employees and Eldercare: Designing Effective Responses for the Workplace* (1989). Dr. Creedon has also published articles on retirement, older workers, and other human-resource issues.

Contents

Foreword

This excellent handbook written by Viola Lechner, DSW, and Michael Creedon, DSW, is a noteworthy addition to the professional literature on the changing needs of families and working caregivers. In view of the growing number of elderly dependents and children, employed caregivers (primarily mothers) face increasingly complex demands. Working parents are often devoted to caring not only for their children, but for an aging parent as well. However, increased work responsibilities make it very difficult for working women and men to care for frail elderly parents, emotionally troubled children or youths, and/or family members with disabilities. This book identifies and discusses the emerging family-sensitive corporate- and government-sponsored programs and employee benefits. The authors describe the full range of workplace responses, including inexpensive child-care referral services, lunchtime seminars and support groups, and intergenerational day-care in the workplace.

Particularly impressive is the authors' focus on policies and programs such as the critically needed federal employee benefit legislation, and the strengths and weaknesses of private vendors. The following are examples of the policies, programs, and issues described in this well-written and informative book:

- The Federal Leave Sharing Act allows federal employees to donate annual leave to a fellow employee so that he or she does not lose income during a family emergency.
- The Family and Medical Leave Act of 1993 requires

employers with 50 or more employees to provide a 12-week leave of absence to employees who have a seriously ill family member, with continuing health and retirement benefits during the leave.

- Over 300 companies have hired work–family coordinators with MBA or MSW degrees to add child-care and elder-care expertise to the employee-assistance program staff.
- Public–private partnerships are being initiated, such as the Partnership for Eldercare developed by the New York City Office on Aging in collaboration with American Express, Morgan Stanley, and Phillip Morris.
- Flextime, flex-place, job sharing, and compressed work weeks have been implemented by a growing number of companies in order to improve employee morale and productivity. Flexible work schedules frequently allow two-career families to juggle responsibilities for child care or elder care more easily, and thereby reduce leave time.
- A consortia of companies and office parks are offering day-care centers for children of employees at a building adjacent to the office complex.
- Not-for-profit agencies such as Catholic Charities and Jewish Family and Children Services are providing geriatric care management for long-distance caregivers. While the aforementioned agencies charge for services on a sliding scale, private geriatric care management companies charge $60 to $150 per hour for their services.
- Lechner and Creedon delineated a seven-step program-development model for labor unions and companies interested in planning and implementing family-focused workplace programs.

This latest addition to the Springer Series on Social Work is a timely and significant contribution to the realities of two important fields—Social Policy and Services, and Occupational Social Work. *Managing Work and Family Life* stands out as an up-to-date, systematic, lucid, and practical text. This authoritative handbook should be purchased by all occupational social workers, vice-presidents of human resources, personnel directors, social work educators, policy analysts, insurance company executives, program supervisors, and reference and acquisitions librarians. It will prove to be an indispensible reference to all practitioners concerned with family and workplace issues and controversies of the 1990s.

ALBERT R. ROBERTS, DSW
Professor and Founding Editor
Springer Series on Social Work

Preface

Almost half of all workers care for dependent children, persons with disabilities, and/or frail elderly relatives. For many, successfully managing twin roles of worker and caregiver is difficult. At the same time, work organizations are very dependent on the commitment and talents of employees, particularly in an era of corporate restructuring and downsizing. Thus, employee satisfaction and well-being is important to success in business. Our society needs an increase in capital investment; it is our thesis that investment in working caregivers is also an essential element of an economic strategy for the 90s.

Major institutions in the United States are beginning to respond to the changing needs of families and working caregivers. Many large companies now provide benefits and services targeted to working caregivers. Some unions are negotiating for family benefits in their joint labor–management contracts. State and federal governing bodies have passed legislation that assists family members. The most recent is the Family and Medical Leave Act of 1993. Numerous profit, not-for-profit, and public vendors offer an array of dependent care services. Public–private partnerships are cropping up as cost-effective measures to solve work and family concerns.

Although much has happened, the United States has miles to go. Workplace, union, government, and community agency assistance to employed caregivers is distributed unevenly throughout the United States. And those currently receiving help need more. The authors hope to aid this process by providing a thorough review of the work and family issues, drawing attention to innovative responses to work and family care dilemmas, recommending ways to improve these responses, and identifying future agendas in this field.

Chapter 1 summarizes the major demographic, social, and economic changes that affect the work and family domains. Connections are made between specific changes and their impact on families, workplaces, community service arrangements, and government policies.

Chapter 2 describes characteristics of the caregivers of children, disabled adults, and elderly persons. Issues discussed include caregiver profiles, work stress, personal stress, work productivity, employer costs of employee caregiver roles, and family care service gaps.

Chapter 3 presents special caregiving situations, including single parents, male caregivers, minority caregivers, gay and lesbian caregivers, and long-distance caregivers. Their particular experiences and needs are discussed.

Chapter 4 presents an overview of family-focused benefits and services that have been adopted by corporations, unions, public, and not-for-profit organizations. They include flexible work arrangements, child care services, elder care services, family leaves, financial assistance programs, educational seminars, counseling, and resource and referral services. Low-cost options for small companies, including consortium arrangements, are highlighted. The phases of company progression from simple awareness of work and family issues to a full integration of workplace changes are described.

Chapter 5 describes the history, structure, and function of employee assistance programs (EAPs) and member assistance programs (MAPs). The strengths and weaknesses of these programs in responding to employed family members are analyzed. Recommendations are offered on ways to strengthen the capacity of EAPs and MAPs to respond to employed persons with family duties.

Chapter 6 describes the roles of the profit and not-for-profit dependent care vendors. Many small and large businesses have cropped up to serve the needs of working families and concerned corporations. The services they provide range from child care centers to national elder care resource and referral phone lines.

Chapter 7 discusses joint corporate and union response

to work and family issues. Several recent labor–management contracts offer innovative solutions to workers' family care strains. These workplace changes are described. Suggestions are given on ways to apply these models to future labor–management negotiations.

Chapter 8 describes relevant public–private partnerships. Increasingly, corporations and both public and voluntary agencies are developing collaborative approaches to caregiving needs of employees. These partnerships range from collaborative research to joint training programs, workplace seminars, and partnerships for intergenerational day care centers.

Chapter 9 describes six steps to implementing family-focused benefits and services: conducting an employee needs assessment, setting up a work and family task force, developing a strategic plan, implementing these plans, training supervisors, and evaluating the work and family programs. A comprehensive employee needs assessment is included in Appendix B.

Chapter 10 summarizes the major ideas presented in the book and proposes an agenda for future directions in the work and family area.

Acknowledgments

The authors thank Bradley Googins and Paul Kurzman for their comments on an earlier draft of the chapter on EAPs; Donna Dolan, Nancy True, and Judith Wineman for their comments on the draft chapter on unions; Lisa May and Stella Strazdas for their assistance on our section on EAP models; and Arthur Emlen for permission to use the "Employee Survey." We also thank the following organizations for their help in locating much needed resources: American Association of Retired Persons, Children's Defense Fund, Families and Work Institute, International Foundation of Employee Benefit Plans, the General Accounting Office, the Urban Institute, U.S. Bureau of the Census, and U.S. Department of Labor. We are grateful to our family, friends, and colleagues for their support throughout the book-writing process.

1 Work and Family Life: A Changing Landscape

This chapter covers the major demographic, social, and economic changes related to work and family issues. It also examines the impact of these changes on the family, the workplace, government, and community service agencies. Reasons are given for the inevitability of greater involvement from work organizations, community agencies, and the government in work and family care dilemmas.

FACT ONE: WORKPLACES ARE VERY DEPENDENT ON FEMALE EMPLOYEES

Women's commitment to the labor force is strong and stable. As shown in Figure 1.1, female employment rates have steadily increased since 1960. In 1992 (U.S. Department of Labor, 1993), 57.8% of women 16 and over were employed, compared to 37.7 in 1960 (U.S. Bureau of the Census, 1986). Additionally, the historic differences between female ethnic groups is closing. The employment rates among white women are catching up with rates for black women, and Hispanic women are catching up with all other ethnic groups. In 1990, 57.8% of black women, 57.5% of white women, 56.7% for Asian women, and 53.0% of Hispanic origin women were in the labor force (Fullerton, 1991).

Workplaces in the near future will be comprised of almost as many women as men. By the year 2005, 47.4% of the work

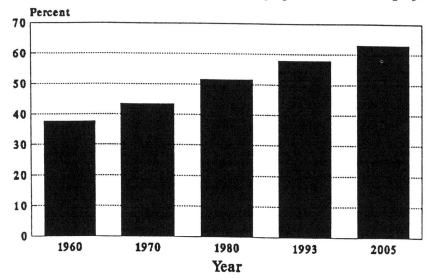

Sources: U.S. Dept. of Labor, 1993; Fullerton, 1991; U.S. Bureau of Census, 1986.

FIGURE 1.1   Female employment rates, 1960 to 2005.

force will be women and 52.6% will be men (Fullerton, 1991). Almost 80% of women age 25 to 54, the most likely caregivers to children and frail adults, will be in the labor force by the turn of the century (National Commission on Working Women, 1989).

Implications

The composition of the labor force is radically changing. It is becoming far more diverse than ever before. With fewer white males to employ and to retain, work organizations are increasingly dependent on ethnically diverse female employees. So employers are put in a position where their success may depend on their ability to hire and to retain female employees. This increased dependency on female workers also calls forth a re-evaluation of current workplace benefits and services originally designed for male employees whose wives were at home.

Changes in the composition of the labor force also affect the type and structure of community services. With more women working, there is greater reliance on paid services to the home: housekeeping, meal preparation, child care, and other forms of dependent care services.

FACT TWO: FAMILIES ARE INCREASINGLY DEPENDENT ON THE FEMALE'S INCOME

Family composition and work force involvement have a major impact on family income. In 1992, the median income of married couples with a working wife was $51,092, compared to $28,408 for families with the woman at home. A working wife almost doubles the family's income. Families headed by women, an increasingly common family type, had the lowest family income—$15,953 in 1992 (U.S. Department of Labor, 1993).

Implications

Working has become, for most families, an economic necessity, rather than a choice. The spiraling costs of housing and higher education coupled with the decline in the actual value of take home pay strongly affect decisions related to employment. Women tend to enter the work force earlier and to stay in, even when their children are very young. Dual-earner families most often work to maintain their middle-class status, while female headed families struggle to maintain a subsistence level.

Working caregivers have limited disposable incomes to purchase child and elder care services. Some employed caregivers have quit their jobs because they were unable to afford dependent care services. Government and workplace programs that help offset the costs of dependent care can enable more caregivers to stay in the work force.

FACT THREE: MOST CHILDREN HAVE WORKING PARENTS

Most of the nation's children under 18 years of age live with parents who work. According to the U.S. Department of Labor, in March, 1992, 65.7% of mothers and fathers, in two parent families, both worked. In female single-parent families, 67%

of the mothers worked. And in male single parent families, 90.5% of the fathers worked (H. Hayghe, personal communication, September 29, 1993).

Eighty percent of employed women are expected to become pregnant during their working life (Fullerton, 1991). In the past, many of these women would have stayed home. But, as shown in Figure 1.2, by the time the child reached one year, 53% of the mothers in 1990 returned to work, compared to only 15% in 1965 (U.S. Bureau of the Census, 1990, 1992). Women's labor force participation rates increase as children grow older. In 1990, 59% of mothers with preschoolers (children under six) worked, whereas 74% of the mothers with school-aged children were in the labor force (U.S. Bureau of the Census, 1992).

Implications

Children's basic needs for care and supervision do not change with the employment practices of family members. Most child experts believe that the quality of care children receive affects their overall well-being. This in turn affects their ability to contribute as adults to work organizations and other aspects of society (Zigler & Lang, 1991). Unfortunately, many older infants and toddlers are in less than adequate child care settings, according to the National Child Care Staffing Study (Zigler & Lang, 1991). And many school-aged children are left to care for themselves while their parents work. Provision of affordable high-quality child care to *all* working parents is one of the major issues facing our society. Such arrangements will take cooperative efforts between corporations, unions, government, and child care providers.

FACT FOUR: WORKING FAMILY MEMBERS CARE FOR A GROWING NUMBER OF ELDERLY PERSONS

The number of persons 65 years old and over is expected to increase in the coming years, at first gradually from 1995 to 2005 and then rapidly from 2010 to 2030, as shown in Figure 1.3 (U.S. Bureau of the Census, 1989). By the year 2030, one in five Americans will be over the age of 65.

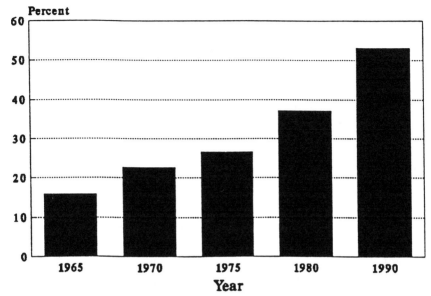

Source: U.S. Bureau of Census, 1990, 1992.

FIGURE 1.2 Women returning to work less than one year after birth of first child, 1965 to 1990.

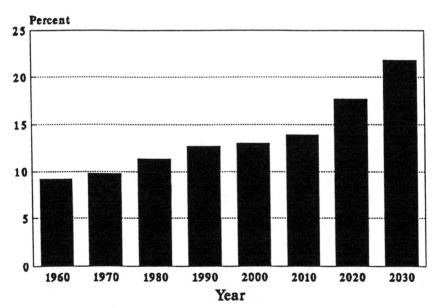

Source: U.S. Bureau of Census, 1989.

FIGURE 1.3 Population age 65 and over, 1960 to 2030.

Implications

Aging increases the likelihood of need for assistance with everyday activities. Only 10% of those aged 65 to 74 need help, compared to 45% for persons over 85 years old (U.S. Bureau of the Census, 1991). Although healthier life styles and better health care have improved the health status of many seniors, the absolute number of older persons in need of assistance will increase (Manton, Corder, & Stallard, 1993). At least 81% of the care for the noninstitutionalized aged comes from relatives, rather than paid helpers (U.S. Congress, House of Representatives, 1987).

While the number of older persons in need of assistance is increasing, the number of at-home family members is decreasing. Women, the traditional caregivers, are often in the work force. Because of the general aging of the population, half of all women in the labor force by the year 2000 will be between the ages of 35 and 54 (U.S. Department of Labor, 1988b). Because many women begin caring for older relatives in their early forties, the number of women who combine work and older relative care is likely to increase (American Association of Retired Persons, 1989; Wagner, Creedon, Sasala, & Neal, 1989).

The National Study of the Changing Workforce estimates that 7% of the U.S. work force care for frail elders and an additional 18% expect to have this responsibility in the near future (Galinsky, Bond, & Friedman, 1993).

With women postponing childbirth, more employed persons will care for the young and the old at the same time. This group is referred to as the "sandwich generation." Furthermore, because of increased longevity, some employees will care for parents as well as for grandparents.

Implications

Families want to care for their aged. However, they also have increased work responsibilities which can make it difficult for them to manage their twin roles. Most employed caregivers would like assistance with their caregiving tasks.

Currently, the service needs of most older persons are not covered or regulated by Medicare, the federal health insurance program for persons over the age of 65. Without adequate funding and reasonable regulation, elder care services become costly and, in many cases, of dubious quality. Like child care services, elder care services are labor intensive and require an ethical, trained work force. It is difficult for dependent care agencies specializing in the long-term care needs of the elderly, to hire, train, and retain quality staff when pay scales must be kept low to remain competitive. Coming to terms with the cost and quality of long-term care services for the growing number of senior citizens will be a major societal issue of the 21st century. Corporations and unions can play a vital role in developing legislation that insures adequate and affordable health and social services for our older citizens.

FACT FIVE: THE NUMBER OF EMPLOYEES CARING FOR DISABLED CHILDREN AND ADULTS IS LIKELY TO INCREASE

The data on the number of employees who work and care for the disabled are scanty. The Census Bureau first began systematically reporting on persons 15 years old and over in need of assistance with everyday activities in 1986. With the passage of the 1990 Americans with Disabilities Act, we hope more attention will be given to this understudied group. Persons with disabilities include people of all ages who have medical and/or mental disabilities and who require assistance with everyday activities.

Demographic data suggest that the adult disabled population has almost doubled in size since 1979. *The National Health Interview Survey* conducted in 1979 (Feller, 1983) found that two million persons 18 to 64 years old needed help with everyday activities, whereas a 1986 survey found that 3.8 million persons 15 to 64 years old needed assistance (U.S. Bureau of the Census, 1991). Advances in medical care that prolong the life of persons with disabilities offers one possible explanation for the increase in the number of disabled adults.

Another explanation may be changes in data collection methods.

Regarding disabled children and youth, the number served by the education system has grown by one million since 1977, going from 3.7 to 4.7 million, an increase of 26.4% (U.S. Department of Education, 1991). Several reasons account for this increase: federal changes in categories of children with disabilities, program development and implementation, and most recently the number of pregnant women who use alcohol and/or other drugs.

One study of employed persons found that 3% of their caregiver sample cared for disabled adults between the ages of 18 and 59 (Neal, Chapman, Ingersoll-Dayton, Emlen, & Boise, 1990). Preliminary findings from a survey of 80,000 federal employees corroborate this figure (U.S. Office of Personnel Management, 1992).

Implications

Data gleaned thus far suggest that the number of persons with disabilities is a fast growing dependent population. More research, however, is needed to determine with greater accuracy the number of persons who both work and care for disabled children and adults. This information is needed to determine the support needs of employed persons, and to further understand the particular pressures parents, spouses, and other relatives who care for the disabled experience.

FACT SIX: WORK ORGANIZATIONS ARE FACING SLOW GROWTH IN PRODUCTIVITY

Productivity expresses the relationship between the quantity of goods and services produced (output) and the quantity of labor, capital, land, energy, and other resources that produced it (input). This relationship is commonly referred to as the amount of output per hour per worker. Although the United States still leads the world in output per worker, our rates of growth in productivity slowed after 1973. Annual productivity growth averaged 2.7% for the period 1960–1973, 0.6% from 1973–1979, and 1.3% from 1979–1987 (U.S. Department of Labor, 1988a). Productivity is the key to improved living standards, corporate wealth, and economic strength.

A number of factors influence productivity: the number of workers, the worker's efficiency and attitude, the quality of available capital (e.g., services or equipment used in product development), and other resources. Work organizations are experiencing much pressure to increase productivity, increase market shares, and reduce costs in order to remain competitive in the global economy. These pressures exist within a context of a U.S. work force in which 47% care for dependents—children, ill spouses or partners, or elders (Galinsky et al., 1993).

Implications

Workers are more interested in the quality of their work life and its effect on family life than they are in monetary rewards, according to the *National Study of the Changing Workforce* (Galinsky et al., 1993). Work organizations wishing to attract and keep valued employees with family responsibilities need to develop policies, benefits, and services that are responsive to their needs. Recent studies show responsive programs make a difference. Johnson & Johnson's and Fel Pro's evaluations of their work–family programs found these programs increased employee loyalty and job satisfaction and decreased job turnover (Families and Work Institute, 1993; Lambert, 1993). These factors are related to increased work productivity.

Even when work organizations downsize, the Families and Work Institute reports, existing work–family programs are retained and new ones are implemented. It is important for companies to offer the "survivors" desirable packages to help increase their morale (Galinsky, Friedman, & Hernandez, 1991). Thus, under conditions of expansion or contraction, family sensitive workplace benefits and services are good business.

REFERENCES

American Association of Retired Persons. (1989). *Working caregivers report: A national survey of caregivers*. Washington, DC: Author.

Families and Work Institute. (1993). *An evaluation of Johnson & Johnson's work and family initiative*. New York: Author.

Feller, B. A. (1983). Americans needing help to function at home. *Advancedata, 92*, 1–3.

Fullerton, H., Jr. (1991). Labor force projections: The baby boom moves on. *Monthly Labor Review, 114*(9), 31–44.

Galinsky, E., Bond, J. T., & Friedman, D. E. (1993). *Highlights: The National Study of the Changing Workforce*. New York: Families and Work Institute.

Galinsky, E., Friedman, D. E., & Hernandez, C. A. (1991). *The corporate reference guide to work-family programs*. New York: Families and Work Institute.

Lambert, S. J. (1993). *Added benefits: The link between family responsive policies and work performance at Fel-Pro Incorporated*. Chicago, IL: University of Chicago.

Manton, K. G., Corder, L. S., & Stallard, E. (1993). Estimates of change in chronic disability and institutional incidence and prevalence rates in the U.S. elderly population from the 1982, 1984, and 1989 National Long Term Care Survey. *Journal of Gerontology, 48*, S153–S166.

National Commission on Working Women. (1989). *Women, work and the future*. Washington, DC: Author.

Neal, M. B., Chapman, N., Ingersoll-Dayton, B., Emlen, A., & Boise, L. (1990). Absenteeism and stress among employed caregivers of the elderly, disabled adults, and children. In D. E. Biegel & A. Blum (Eds.), *Aging and caregiving: Theory, research, and policy* (pp. 160–183). CA: Sage.

U.S. Bureau of the Census. (1986). *Women in the American economy* (Current Population Reports, Series P-23, No. 146). Washington, DC: U.S. Government Printing Office.

U.S. Bureau of the Census. (1989). *Projections of the population of the United States by age, sex, and race: 1988 to 2080* (Current Population Reports, Series P-25, No. 1018). Washington, DC: U.S. Government Printing Office.

U.S. Bureau of the Census. (1990). *Work and family patterns of American women* (Current Population Reports, Series P-23, No. 165). Washington, DC: U.S. Government Printing Office.

U.S. Bureau of the Census. (1991). *Population profile of the United*

States: 1991 (Current Population Reports, Series P-23, No. 173). Washington, DC: U.S. Government Printing Office.

U.S. Bureau of the Census. (1992). *Household, families, and children: A 30 year perspective* (Current Population Reports, Series P-23, No. 181). Washington, DC: U.S. Government Printing Office.

U.S. Congress, House of Representatives. (1987). *Exploring the myths: Caregiving in America* (Select Committee on Aging, Comm. Pub. No. 99-611). Washington, DC: U.S. Government Printing Office.

U.S. Department of Education. (1991). *To assure the free appropriate public education of all children with disabilities: Thirteenth annual report to Congress on the implementation of the Individuals with Disabilities Education Act.* Washington, DC: U.S. Government Printing Office.

U.S. Department of Labor, Bureau of Labor Statistics. (1993). *Employment and earnings.* Washington, DC: U.S. Government Printing Office.

U.S. Department of Labor, Bureau of Labor Statistics. (1988a). *Productivity and the economy: A chartbook,* (Bulletin 2298). Washington, DC: U.S. Government Printing Office.

U.S. Department of Labor, Women's Bureau. (1988b). *Facts on U.S. working women.* Washington, DC: U.S. Government Printing Office.

U.S. Office of Personnel Management. (1992, April). *The study of the work and family needs of the federal workforce: A report to Congress.* Washington, DC: Office of Work and Family, U.S. Office of Personnel Management.

Wagner, D. L., Creedon, M. C., Sasala, J. M., & Neal, M. B. (1989). *Employees and eldercare: Designing effective responses for the workplace.* Bridgeport, CT: University of Bridgeport.

Zigler, E. F., & Lang, M. E. (1991). *Child care choices: Balancing the needs of children, families, and society.* New York: The Free Press.

2 The Caregivers

Molley, a 35-year-old secretary, has just dropped off her 3-year-old at a child care center near her home. She got up at 6 A.M. in order to get everyone else up, fix their breakfasts, prepare their lunches and her own. She was almost late for work. Her boss has warned her about further tardiness. As she approaches her desk, she has many worries. One is about her daughter getting enough individualized attention at the child care center. Another concern is getting to the center before it closes today—she is expected to stay late if a customer comes in. She is also frustrated with her husband's lack of awareness of her many responsibilities.

Sam, a 55-year-old civil engineer works as a foreman for a large factory. He is worried about his wife of 26 years who had a stroke a year ago. While at work, he worries about his wife's isolation and loneliness and is fearful she might fall out of the wheelchair. Before he goes to work, he helps her bathe, prepares her breakfast, and sets aside a sandwich for her lunch. He could use a home health aide, but his insurance doesn't cover this service.

Mary, a 48-year-old manager, is devoted to her 80-year-old mother, who needs a fair amount of help with everyday activities. Like Molley and Sam, she gets up early. Each day is a busy one. Before work, she takes the subway to her mother's house to fix her breakfast. During her lunch hour, she returns again to prepare lunch and to just chat. After work, she returns to her mother's house to fix her dinner and to help her bathe. Mary is tired. Three years is a long time to keep up this pace.

Mary, Sam, and Molley express many of the common and unique struggles working caregivers face on a daily basis. They also represent 47% of the U.S. work force who make substantial contributions to society through their commitment to their jobs and to their loved ones.

This chapter describes the experiences of employees caring for children, the disabled, and the frail elderly. It also looks at the impact of managing these joint roles on employees themselves, their family members, and their workplaces.

EMPLOYEES CARING FOR CHILDREN

The National Study of the Changing Workforce estimates that 42% of the work force have responsibilities for the care of children under the age of 18 (Galinsky, Bond, & Friedman, 1993). Employees with these tasks are very busy people—frequently working the equivalent of *two* fulltime jobs on work, household chores, and child care (Galinsky et al., 1993; Burden & Googins, 1987). Employed mothers are the busiest. In the *National Study of the Changing Workforce* (Galinsky et al., 1993), 71% of employed women compared to 5% of men indicated they had primary responsibility for care of children. Fernandez (1990) notes, however, based on his 1984 and 1988 studies of employed parents, that men are taking on more home and child care chores.

Men and women often differ in the types of child care tasks they perform. Men generally get involved in fun with their children and in nonroutine tasks that easily can be incorporated into their daily lives. Women, on the other hand, generally take care of daily tasks that bind them to rigid schedules. Also, working mothers respond to crisis situations more often than employed fathers. They are more likely to stay home from work to accommodate a failed child care arrangement or to take care of a sick child (Fernandez, 1990).

Child Care Arrangements

According to two nationally representative studies, locating high-quality child care and paying for it are working parents most pressing concerns (Galinsky et al., 1993; Hofferth, Brayfield, Deich, & Holcomb, 1991). It takes about seven weeks for a parent to find suitable child care. Once found, high income families spend 6% of their family income on child care and low income families spend a whopping 25% (Hofferth et al., 1991).

The National Research Council (1990), a well-known bipartisan research organization, concluded that "a number of children are in settings that do not protect their health and safety and do not provide appropriate developmental stimulation. Poor quality care, more than any single type of program or arrangement, threatens children's development, especially children from poor and minority families" (p. xii). National standards and reasonable regulations would help improve the quality of child care throughout the U.S.

Employed parents use a variety of child care arrangements: center-based care (group care for 12 or more children in commercial buildings), family day care (group care for approximately 6 children in providers' homes), in-home providers (care in employees' own homes by nannies, fulltime babysitters, etc.), relative care; and after school lessons. Child care arrangements break down fairly frequently. In *The National Study of the Changing Workforce*, 32% of parents of children under the age of five and 20% of parents with children 5 to 12 years old reported a breakdown in the preceding three months (Galinsky et al., 1993).

Women report more work–family interferences, more personal stress and unwanted health changes, and more limitations in career advancement than do men (Emlen, 1990; Fernandez, 1990; Galinsky, Friedman, & Hernandez, 1991). This is not surprising given their greater involvement in home and family caregiving tasks. When employed fathers assume as much responsibility as mothers for child and home chores, they also show similar levels of personal stress (Burden & Googins, 1987). Fernandez (1990) notes that with men taking on more home and child care chores they are beginning to catch up with women in reporting child care problems and personal stress, according to his 1984 and 1988 studies of employed parents. Parents of both sexes report that among the unpredictable events, the care of the sick child creates the most work–family interference (Fernandez, 1990; Galinsky et al., 1991).

Some children (approximately 7 to 10 million or more) take care of themselves, receiving no adult supervision (Hofferth et al., 1991; Zigler & Lang, 1991). They are known as the "latchkey kids." The *National Child Care Survey, 1990* reports the number of children 13 and younger without adult supervision has doubled since 1984 (Hofferth et al., 1991).

In addition to daily supervision, employed parents cite the following concerns: managing unpredictable crises (e.g., child becomes ill or the babysitter becomes sick), finding child care during school vacations and holidays, going to school conferences, and scheduling medical appointments (Fernandez, 1990).

Impact of Managing Work and Child Care

The Families and Work Institute's surveys of thousands of employees reveal that 40% of employed parents experience difficulty managing their job and family responsibilities (Galinsky et al., 1991). As a matter of fact, employees caring for children reported more financial stress and more difficulty managing work and family tasks than those caring for disabled adults or frail elders (Neal, Chapman, Ingersoll-Dayton, & Emlen, 1993). This section explores how combining work and care of children affects employed parents and their children.

Health outcomes. Fernandez (1990) found a significant relationship between parents' reported child care problems and stress related health problems. In a national study of employed parents, those experiencing breakdowns in their child care arrangements reported feeling nervous or stressed twice as often as employed parents with no problems (Galinsky, 1987). Furthermore, these child care problems were significantly related to stress-related health problems, such as shortness of breath, back or neck pains, overeating, smoking, increased alcohol consumption, and increased use of tranquilizers. Men and women experiencing high levels of work-family role strain report higher levels of depression (Burden & Googins, 1987). *The National Study of the Changing Workforce* found that parents with fewer child care breakdowns and reasonable child care expenses were more satisfied with their lives, less stressed, and better able to cope as parents (Galinsky et al., 1993).

Family tensions. Arlie Hochschild's qualitative study of dual earner couples with children found that women's greater involvement in home and child care tasks contributed to tensions between the parents and tensions within the family (1989). Women resented their lion's share of the work and the resentment came out in arguments between the spouses and in crankiness with the children. The result, Hochschild suggests, is that nobody wins when one parent assumes more than a fair share.

Studies of employed parents indicate that parents' stress levels tend to decrease as the age of the child increases (Emlen, 1990; Fernandez, 1990). A possible reason is that the effort, time, and cost of child care diminish as children grow and become less dependent on their parents and other caregivers.

Effect of employment on children. Several prominent child care experts have reported the controversial findings that fulltime day care, as opposed to having a parent at home, may harm children under the age of one (Zigler & Lang, 1991). Harmful effects are related to inadequate bonding between mother and child and low quality child care services.

The second major concern among child care experts is latch key kids. Research on the effects of self-care on children is limited and inconclusive. However, two studies report that unsupervised children are more susceptible to peer pressure to engage in undesirable behavior including drug use, criminal acts, and sexual activity (Seligson & Fink, 1989). The National Institute of Child Health and Human Development started a 5-year study in 1990 to answer questions related to the long-term impact of employment on children's lives. There has been a dearth of such longitudinal research.

Service requests. Among working parents the most frequently requested services are good quality, affordable child care services and flexible work arrangements. The ideal support for most parents would be environments that enable them to be available to their children when they need them the most. Zigler, a prominent child psychologist and one of the creators of the universally popular Head Start Program, suggests that parents, mothers in particular, should be allowed to remain at home with their infants below the age of one (Zigler & Lang, 1991). This precludes full-time but not part-time work. He believes this amount of time is needed for the family unit to become safe and nurturing for the infant. He further states that we can expect more troubled youth if we do not provide them with the minimum level of a healthy environment. If we do not invest in our children in the beginning, we will lose in the future, for they will not be prepared for the tasks of work and family life.

EMPLOYEES CARING FOR ELDERS

The caregiving needs of the elderly, unlike those of children, are frequently impossible to predict and to plan for. Some older persons may never need assistance, while others may need considerable help for a long period of time. Even if the frail relative enters a nursing home, caregiving tasks do not cease. Oftentimes relatives supervise the nursing home care, do the elder's laundry, and perform other personal chores, in addition to visiting as often as possible. Some employees may care for only one relative, while others may care for several relatives at the same time or at different times over a number of years. *The National Study of the Changing Workforce* found that 77% of caregivers cared for only one elder and 23% cared for two or more elders (Galinsky et al., 1993).

The older persons's need for assistance can vary widely

from periodic transportation assistance to continuous home health care. The elderly generally become more dependent as the years pass and need more care. Adult care can be marked by much ambivalence regarding the caregiving commitment. Feelings of affection toward the care receiver may vary a lot (especially among daughters-in-law) and the attitude of the elder may be a crucial factor, also (Lechner, 1991). These descriptions are in marked contrast to child care experiences in which tasks are specific to the age of the children and tasks decline with the children's increased independence.

Characteristics of Employed Caregivers for the Elderly

The National Study of the Changing Workforce estimates that 7% of workers care for persons 50 years old and over and an additional 18% expect to take on this responsibility in the next five years (Galinsky et al., 1993). Employed caregivers include executives as well as laborers (*Fortune Magazine* and John Hancock Financial Services, 1989). They are relatively young —many begin caregiving in their late thirties and early forties (Wagner, Creedon, Sasala, & Neal, 1989).

Studies of working caregivers reveal they spend an average of 6 to 12 hours a week on elder care tasks (American Association of Retired Persons [AARP], 1989; Galinsky et al., 1993; Wagner et al., 1989). However, caregiving hours can increase to as much as 35 hours per week for very impaired relatives (Brody, Kleban, Johnsen, Hoffman, & Schoonover, 1987; Gibeau, Anastas, & Larson, 1987; Petty & Friss, 1987). The primary type of care that is provided is maintenance care (transporting, shopping and household chores), rather than personal care (feeding and dressing) (AARP, 1989; Gibeau et al., 1987; Scharlach & Boyd, 1989). The average years spent in elder care range from five and one-half years to almost seven years (Petty & Friss, 1987; Wagner et al., 1989).

Most studies indicate that 75% of caregivers are women (AARP, 1989; Gorey, Rice, & Brice, 1990). However, *The National Study of the Changing Workforce* found a very different situation—54% of caregivers to the elderly were women and 46% were men (Galinsky et al., 1993). All studies concur, however, that men generally provide maintenance assistance, rather than the more labor-intensive and emotionally taxing personal care.

Impact of Providing Care

Seventy percent of working caregivers report that their work and family duties interfere with each other (Bureau of National Affairs, 1988). Emotional strain is the most frequently reported negative consequence (Brody et al., 1987; Gibeau et.al., 1987; Neal et al., 1993; Scharlach & Boyd, 1989).

Health outcomes. One study of employees at three corporations found that caregiving duties affected the employed caregiver's health (Creedon, 1987). Employed caregivers had three times as many problems with anxiety and depression and twice as many headaches as employees without caregiving duties.

Thus far, the research literature suggests that two aspects of the employee caregiver's life best predict caregiver strain: the number of work interferences (unscheduled days off, late arrivals, early departures, and excessive telephone use related to the older relative), and the level of the dependent person's impairment (Lechner, 1993; Scharlach, Sobel, and Roberts, 1991). These predictors are connected; the most-disabled parents, needing the most time and attention, most affect the employees' ability to get to work on time and stick to their work schedule. Those employees with the most caregiving demands report the most strain. Females report the most work interferences (Neal et al., 1993).

Service needs. Employed caregivers to the elderly most frequently request information and referral services, personal counseling, lunch time seminars, and long-term care insurance (Lechner, 1991; Neal et al., 1993; Scharlach & Boyd, 1989). Among existing services at the workplace, flexible hours and use of personal time for family illness were the most helpful (Scharlach & Boyd, 1989).

Attitudes affect utilization of workplace elder care programs. Caregivers wishing to keep family matters separate from work matters use fewer workplace programs (Wagner & Hunt, 1992). Those who do not think of themselves as "caregivers" do not look for or seek out elder care programs.

EMPLOYEES CARING FOR CHILDREN AND ELDERLY RELATIVES

According to a national study, 1% of the workforce are responsible for the care of both children and frail elders (Stone & Kemper, 1989). However, two smaller workplace surveys reveal a much greater frequency of overlap—42% of caregivers of elders also have child care responsibilities in both studies (Fairfax Area Agency on Aging, 1991; Neal et al., 1993). Whatever the exact number, this group of caregivers, often referred to as the "sandwich generation," is expected to increase in size due to longer life expectancy and the current delay in childbearing (Stone, Cafferata, & Sangl, 1987).

Impact of Providing Care

Employed persons with child and elder care responsibilities report more personal and work-related strain than employed persons who care only for elders or for children (Fernandez, 1990; Neal et al., 1993). In certain situations, though, these dependent care tasks can be less stressful, rather than more stressful (Fernandez, 1990). For example, less frail elders can help with child care assistance, especially when children become sick or the child care arrangement breaks down. Older children and/or a larger number of children might increase the number of available helpers to the frail elders.

EMPLOYEES CARING FOR PERSONS WITH DISABILITIES

Persons with disabilities can be any age and their condition can be chronic or acute, although most tend to be the former. Disabilities can include physical, emotional, and cognitive impairments. A short list of disabilities may include mental retardation, schizophrenia, hearing and vision impairment, stroke sequelae, AIDS, and genetic illnesses such as muscular dystrophy. Some disabled persons can lead fairly independent lives, while others need constant medical and personal care.

Children with Disabilities

Employed parents of children with disabilities are a very diverse group. For some, their child's medical condition worsens with age; for others, the condition will stay the same or even improve as the child grows older.

Information is limited on employees who care for disabled children. Fernandez's studies of employed caregivers (1990) found that 10% of the study population cared for disabled children, and this group reported more stress, more difficulty finding appropriate child care, and an increased likelihood to have considered staying home with their children than other employed parents.

The Center for Social Policy and Practice in the Workplace at Columbia University School of Social Work found that 8% of the union members they surveyed had a handicapped child. This group scored high on work interferences such as missing work, arriving late, and leaving early (Krauskopf & Akabas, 1988).

We can assume that women are generally the caregivers of disabled children and that male partners' assistance, when present, resembles their assistance in the care of well children and frail older persons. Employed parents caring for disabled children must deal with the usual developmental issues plus the additional responsibilities of medical care and supervision, depending on the type of disability. They may face lifelong caregiving, particularly if they care for a child with a chronic disability, since the child may never reach a level of independence that would enable him or her to live alone.

The two most critical issues for employed caregivers may be the length of time spent giving care and the difficulty in finding appropriate services, including emotional and practical support (Bureau of National Affairs, 1991).

Zigler and Lang (1991) poignantly describe the life of working parents of children with special needs. In many cases they are the most vulnerable of employed caregivers in terms of emotional and financial strain. Most need to work to keep their insurance and to pay for their child's medical and social services, yet locating appropriate, affordable services can be most difficult.

Prejudices and fears about those who are different, the limited number of caregivers with specialty training, and a host of geographic, physical, and legislative requirements set up imposing barriers for these families (Bureau of National Affairs, 1991). Thus, the most vulnerable are left to deal with the most difficult child care services and problems. Many child care providers, including employer-supported facilities, do not accept children with disabilities (Bureau of National Affairs, 1991). Some states have laws that prohibit child care facilities from admitting acutely ill children, even if they are able to isolate them from the well children.

Service needs.   In addition to help in obtaining child care services, employed parents also need flexible work schedules and respite care programs. They may need counseling regarding their child's long-term health care needs or their feelings and the family's feelings about the disabled child (Bureau of National Affairs, 1991; Furneaux, 1988; Krauskopf & Akabas, 1988). These programs could help reduce the parents' sense of isolation and of being left alone to struggle with their many problems.

Adults With Disabilities

Two studies on employees caring for adults with disabilities revealed that 3% of the study populations cared for adults 18–60 years old (Neal et al., 1993; U.S. Office of Personnel Management, 1992). Neal and associates' (1993) study of employed caregivers revealed that those caring for disabled adults were most likely to be professional women caring for their parents. These same women were also primary caregivers to their children and had responsibilities to spouses. Among the four employee groups studied (caregivers to elderly, disabled adults, children, and those with no caregiving responsibilities), employees caring for disabled adults reported the most personal health stress.

Employment, however, has been found to offer a respite from caregiving. The Family Survival Project reported that fulltime employed caregivers to brain-impaired persons were less stressed than caregivers to persons with similar diagnoses who did not work or worked parttime (Petty & Friss, 1987). The disabled adults in this study required considerable amounts of assistance and tolerance of their confused and agitated behavior.

EFFECTS OF FAMILY TASKS ON THE WORKPLACE

Current studies suggest that work productivity and employer health care costs are affected by employees' family responsibilities.

Productivity

Productivity measurements are based on (a) employer's success in hiring and retaining workers and (b) workers' ability to perform job tasks promptly and successfully.

Attracting and keeping employees. According to the *National Longitudinal Study of Youth*, an estimated 1.1 million young mothers (ages 21–29) with children under six were out of the labor force in 1986 because of child care problems (Cattan, 1991). This group represents a loss to the workplace in terms of potential new hires. Once hired, however, many employees with dependent family members find it difficult to stay. The *National Child Care Survey* reports that 25% of mothers left their jobs due to family reasons. Other studies reveal that between 9% and 22% of employees caring for the elderly quit their jobs to care for a frail relative (Brody et al., 1987; Cattan, 1991; Petty & Friss, 1987; Stone et al., 1987).

Work performance. Employees' preoccupation about family members while at work and the number of work interferences (late arrivals, early departures, excessive telephoning, and absences) due to family needs negatively affect attention to and participation in job duties. Two studies of employed caregivers found that 69% of employed parents and 94% of employed caregivers to the elderly worried about how their loved ones were doing while they were at work (Burden & Googins; 1987; Lechner, 1991). These distractions can interfere with work tasks.

In a review of numerous studies, the Conference Board found that, on the average, employees arrived late or left early due to child care obligations about 1.8 days every 6 months (Friedman, 1991). Employees with elder care responsibilities also reported frequent work interferences, such as excessive telephoning, work delays, and tardiness because of parent care duties (Brody et al., 1987; Gibeau et al., 1987; Neal et al., 1993; Scharlach & Boyd, 1989; Wagner et al., 1989). Based on a review of numerous studies, the Conference Board found that the average number of days missed for elder care tasks was 7.5 days per year; for child care it was 5.7 days (Friedman, 1991). Absenteeism rates were highest among parents with young children and/or three or more children (Galinsky, 1987). It should be noted, however, that employee absences may actually reduce employee stress. Emlen's research found that companies with low rates of absenteeism had higher percentages of employees who reported stress related to child care (Emlen, 1990). Perhaps when an employee stays home with the sick child or the child whose care arrangement broke down, the parent feels less guilt and frustration about family duties and consequently less stress.

Other Costs to Employers

Based on a survey of 26,000 employees in 30 companies (employing between 50 and 15,000 people), Fernandez (1990) has estimated that the yearly cost to a company for employee absences (related to caregiving responsibilities for children) was $1.8 million, based on average salary plus benefits of $100 per day.

There is growing evidence that managing work and caregiving can negatively affect one's health status, and, as a result, employers' health care costs. The Family Survival Project's study of employed caregivers of brain-impaired adults found this group was 20% more likely to have visited a physician recently than noncaregivers and had much higher rates of stress related illnesses such as depression, sleeplessness, weight gain, and weight loss (Enright and Friss, 1987). Similar stress related illnesses among employed caregivers to the elderly have been reported (Creedon, 1987; Lechner, 1991). Employer health care costs could be adversely affected by these employee illnesses.

FACTORS AFFECTING STRESS

Multiple Roles

Although managing work and family care is stressful for most employed caregivers, under certain conditions, the stress level is reduced. First, for employees caring for disabled children and adults requiring a great deal of help and tolerance, work can provide a break from caregiving (Krauskopf & Akabas; 1988; Enright & Friss, 1987). In this case, the experience in one role may be a buffer against the unwanted affects of another role. Second, the expectations of successful role performance in each role is diminished when many roles are taken on. Third, when the dependent person helps with home or child care tasks, the employed caregiver's work–family conflict may be reduced. For example, as noted earlier, mildly impaired elders are in a position to help care for the worker's children.

Support From Family, Friends, and Supervisors

The literature suggests that support from family, friends, supervisors, church groups, and other networks often limit the negative effects of managing two busy roles (Burden & Googins, 1987; Galinsky et al., 1993; Horowitz, 1985). These groups offer two distinct types of assistance: emotional support and practical help. Emotional support is provided by someone able to talk to the caregiver about personal frustrations regarding the caregiving situation. Practical support includes assistance with the everyday tasks of caregiving. A relative who is available for backup when child care arrangements break down or to take a parent to the doctor's office during the employee's work day is part of the support network. Satisfaction with the help received is more important than the number of helpers (Horowitz, 1985; Seeman, 1992).

Women have a larger number of support persons, but men may benefit more from their support systems. In a longitudinal study of support and health outcomes, men showed positive effects of support on stress buffering while women did not (Seeman, 1992). The researchers surmised that for women the give and take of relationships counterbalanced the capacity of support to buffer stress in time of need.

Longitudinal studies that follow caregivers over time report that the most useful type of support is emotional support during a time of need (Seeman, 1992). These studies did not include employed caregivers who may, in fact, need help with tasks as well as emotional support.

In studies of employed caregivers to the elderly, Lechner (1993) found that support and assistance from family and friends as well as availability of community agencies buffered the negative impact of caregiving and work and family role strain. Scharlach et al. (1991) found that perceived adequacy of support reduced employed caregivers' number of work interferences. Fewer work interferences, in turn, reduced the perceived likelihood of job termination.

Burden and Googins (1987) also report similar findings for employed parents regarding the supervisor's role in decreasing the stressful effects of dual-role demands. Galinsky and associates of the Families and Work Institute (1991) suggest that supportive supervisors can increase work productivity, decrease employee stress, and decrease absenteeism. Specifically, the supervisor's handling of the employee's work–family conflicts is as important as the other tasks the supervisor performs. According to the Institute, the best supervisors are those who see family issues as legitimate concerns, know the company's policies related to family issues, apply those policies without favoritism, and are supportive with everyday as well as emergency work–family problems (Galinsky, 1992).

Work Conditions

Occupational status, income, and flexibility in work schedules have been found to differentially affect employed caregivers. Fernandez (1990) found that upper management women caring for children reported more child care problems than women in other occupational positions. He speculates that these women are in very demanding jobs that make it difficult for them to be available for family crises and children's events that occur during their work hours. Neal and associates' (1993) study of employees in 33 companies found that all employees caring for children, regardless of occupation, reported many work interruptions to take care of family tasks. However, the situation was different for employees caring for frail elders and disabled adults, where nonprofessional employees were more likely than professional employees to report work interruptions.

The Conference Board's review of the literature found that persons in managerial positions were more likely to have demanding jobs that made it difficult to balance their work and family demands, but persons in lower status positions had less flexibility in getting to the phone and receiving calls at work (Friedman, 1991).

Regarding income, caregivers with the highest incomes reported fewer problems combining work and family tasks (Friedman, 1991; Neal et al., 1993). Those in higher income groups were in a better position to purchase services and services of better quality for their children and disabled or frail relatives.

Employees caring for children or frail elders who were in jobs with the least flexibility reported the most difficulty managing work and caregiving tasks (Neal et al., 1993), but also fewer work interferences in another study (Scharlach et al., 1991). For caregivers to elderly parents, a supportive work environment, one that had flexible work policies and an understanding supervisor, lessened their mental strain (Lechner, 1993). Galinsky (1992) also found that of all job conditions assessed (scheduled work hours, overtime, control over scheduling, commuting time, supervisor support, and supportive work policies) the degree of family supportiveness in the work culture was the most significant. Employees who perceived the work environment as unsupportive were the most likely to have stress-related health problems, to worry about their children while at work, and to be concerned about their productivity.

SUMMARY

In summary, the literature suggests the following conclusions:

1. Employment has not decreased family members commitment to dependent persons.
2. Gender differences are evident in many aspects of caregiving. Employed women with children continue to perform most of the home and child care tasks. Although employed men are more involved in the care of frail relatives than in childcare, their participation is primarily limited to the less demanding tasks.
3. Most caregivers have some difficulty managing their joint roles.
4. Managing work and caregiving has costs to employees, their children, disabled relatives, and frail elders, and also to their employers.

Partnerships are needed between men and women, between employees and employers, and between the government and all other bodies in order to provide for two of society's basic tasks—economic production and the care of dependent persons. Future chapters take a look at these pressing issues.

REFERENCES

American Association of Retired Persons. (1989). *Working caregivers report: A national survey of caregivers.* Washington, DC: Author.

Brody, E. M., Kleban, M. H., Johnsen, P. T., Hoffman, C., & Schoonover, C. B. (1987). Work status and parent care: A comparison of four groups of women. *The Gerontologist, 27,* 201–208.

Burden, D. S., & Googins, B. (1987). *Boston University: Balancing job and homelife study.* Boston, MA: Boston University School of Social Work.

Bureau of National Affairs. (1988). *Employers and eldercare: A new benefit coming of age* (Report No. 3). Rockville, MD: Buraff Publications.

Bureau of National Affairs. (1991). *Caring for children with special needs* (Report No. 43). Washington, DC: Author.

Cattan, P. (1991). Child-care problems: An obstacle to work. Monthly *Labor Review, 114*(10), 3–9.

Creedon, M. A. (1987). *Issues for an aging America: Employees and eldercare.* Southport, CT: Creative Services.

Emlen, A. C. (1990). *Work and family: Assessing the balance.* Presentation at National Association of Social Workers Annual Meeting, Boston, MA.

Enright, R. B., & Friss, L. (1987). *Employed caregivers of brain-impaired adults: An assessment of the dual role.* San Francisco, CA: Family Survival Project.

Fairfax Area Agency on Aging. (1991). *The missing worker: Caring for mom and dad.* Fairfax County, VA: Author.

Fernandez, J. P. (1990). *The politics and reality of family care in corporate America.* Lexington, MA: Lexington Books.

Fortune Magazine and John Hancock Financial Services. (1989). *Corporate and employee response to caring for the elderly: A national survey of U.S. companies and the workforce.* New York: The Time Inc. Magazine Company.

Friedman, D. E. (1991). *Linking work-family issues to the bottom line: A summary of research.* New York: The Conference Board.

Furneaux, B. (1988). *Special parents.* Philadelphia: Open University Press.

Galinsky, E. (1987). *The impact of child care problems on parents on the job and at home.* New York: Bank Street College of Education.

Galinsky, E., Bond, J. T., & Friedman, D. E. (1993). *Highlights: The National Study of the Changing Workforce.* New York: Families and Work Institute.

Galinsky, E., Friedman, D. E., & Hernandez, C. A. (1991). *The Corporate reference guide to work-family programs.* New York: Families and Work Institute.

Galinsky, E. (1992). *Harmonizing work and family responsibilities: Research and corporate perspectives.* Presentation at 69th Annual Conference of the American Orthopsychiatric Association, New York.

Gibeau, J. L., Anastas, J. W., & Larson, P. J. (1987). Breadwinners, caregivers and employers: New alliances in an aging America. *Employer Benefits Journal, 12*(3), 6–10.

Gorey, K. M., Rice, R. W., & Brice, G. C. (1992). The prevalence of elder care responsibilities among the work force population: Response bias among a group of cross-sectional surveys. *Research on Aging, 14,* 399–418.

Hochschild, A. (1989). *Second shift.* New York: Viking Penguin.

Hofferth, S. L., Brayfield, A., Deich, S., & Holcomb, P. (1991). *National child care survey,* 1990. Washington, DC: The Urban Institute Press.

Horowitz, A. (1985). Family caregiving to the frail elderly. In M. P. Lawton & G. L. Maddox (Eds.), *Annual review of gerontology and geriatrics: Vol. 5* (pp. 194–246). New York: Springer.

Krauskopf, M. S., & Akabas, S. H. (1988). Children with disabilities: A family/work partnership in problem resolution. *Social Work Papers, 21,* 28–35.

Lechner, V. M. (1991). Predicting future commitment to care for frail parents among employed caregivers. *Journal of Gerontological Social Work, 18,* 69–84.

Lechner, V. M. (1993). Support systems and stress reduction among workers caring for dependent parents. *Social Work, 38,* 461–469.

National Research Council. (1990). *Who cares for America's children?* Washington, DC: National Academy Press.

Neal, M. B., Chapman, N. J., Ingersoll-Dayton, B., & Emlen, A. C. (1993). *Balancing work and caregiving for children, adults, and elders.* CA: Sage.

Petty, D., & Friss, L. (1987). A balancing act of working and caregiving. *Business and Health, 4*(12), 22–26.

Scharlach, A. E., & Boyd, S. (1989). Caregiving and employment: Results of an employee survey. *The Gerontologist, 29,* 382–387.

Scharlach, A. E., Sobel, E. L., & Roberts, R. E. (1991). Employment and caregivers strain: An integrative model. *The Gerontologist, 31,* 778–787.

Seeman, T. (1992). *Social relationships/social support and aging.* Presentation given at Brookdale Foundation & National Institute on Aging, Summer Institute. Warrenton, VI.

Seligson, M., & Fink, D. B. (1989). *No time to waste.* Wellesley, MA: Wellesley College Center for Research on Women.

Stone, R., Cafferata, G. L., & Sangl, J. (l987). Caregivers of the frail elderly: A national profile. *The Gerontologist, 27,* 6l6–626.

Stone, R., & Kemper, P. (1989). Spouses and children of disabled elders: How large a constituency for long-term care reform? *The Milbank Quarterly, 67*, 485–506.

U.S. Office of Personnel Management. (1992, April). The study of the work and family needs of the federal workforce: A report to Congress. Washington, DC: Office of Work and Family, U.S. Office of Personnel Management.

Wagner, D. L., Creedon, M. C., Sasala, J. M., & Neal, M. B. (1989). *Employees and eldercare: Designing effective responses for the workplace.* CT: University of Bridgeport.

Wagner, D. L., & Hunt, G. G. (1992). Factors influencing utilization of workplace programs by employed caregivers. Poster presented at 45th Annual Meeting of Gerontological Society of America, Washington, DC.

Zigler, E. F., & Lang, M. E. (1991). *Child care choices: Balancing the needs of children, families, and society.* New York: The Free Press.

3 Special Caregiving Situations

Chapter 2 discussed many aspects of managing work and family care. In this chapter, we highlight several groups of caregivers that deserve special attention: men, single parents, minorities, nontraditional couples, and long-distance caregivers of frail relatives.

MALE CAREGIVERS

When we think of diversity in the work force does it include working fathers? Although women perform most of the home and child care chores, employed fathers have increased their participation in family duties from 20% in the mid-1960s to 30% in the mid-1980s (Pleck, 1989, 1993). They also have shown modest increases in assuming primary responsibility for the care of their young children while the mother works (Hofferth, Brayfield, Deich, & Holcomb, 1991). Regarding the care of disabled or frail spouses, men have often been the primary caregivers.

Why are men increasing their participation in caregiving? What are their experiences? What is the impact on children and other family members of their involvement? These questions are explored next.

Factors Contributing to Male Caregiving

Michael Lamb (1987) suggests there are at least four conditions that explain employed fathers' participation in the caregiving role: motivation, self-confidence, support from family, and supportive institutional practices. We believe these conditions are also relevant to male caregivers of disabled adults and frail elders.

Motivation. In Arlie Hochschild's book, *Second Shift*, a father spoke with pride and amazement about his equally shared parent role to rambunctious twin boys. "I hadn't imagined the extent of nurturing feelings I have that I had really played down" and "I honestly think I am the best father I know," he told Hochschild. (1989 p. 177).

Parallels are found in the study by Leonard Kaye and Jeffrey Applegate (1990) of males caring for spouses with Alzheimer's disease. They, too, felt pride and loving feelings about their responsibilities. One respondent said, "She's my wife and I love her" and another said, "I've been married to her for so long and I still love her. She was the perfect mate for me" (p. 79).

The men quoted here show a strong desire to be caregivers. Possible reasons for mens' increasing participation in caregiving include: a) the influx of women into the labor force, which decreased their time for family matters and put more pressure on men to help in the home, b) the increase in the number of elderly in need of care coupled with women's decreased availability because of work, c) changes in men's desire to spend more time with their children, d) for men who become caregivers late in life, biopsychosocial changes that promote stronger desires to nurture, and e) the women's movement, which sent out the message to men that women wanted gender roles to be more androgenous.

Self-Confidence. Motivation alone, however, does not guarantee greater involvement of men in the caregiving role. The men in Kaye and Applegate's (1990) study who cared for wives with Alzheimers admitted that their lack of perceived competency with personal care chores (e.g., dressing and bathing) created a barrier for them. It decreased their satisfaction with caregiving and increased their hesitancy to take on these tasks. More open communication with other family members and educational sessions provided through the workplace and community agencies could do much to help men feel more confident in roles they have been less prepared to handle.

Support from family. Besides motivation and self confidence with child care tasks, Lamb (1987), writing about employed fathers, points out that men need to feel that their wives accept their caregiving behavior. His review of several studies indicated that 60% to 80% of wives surveyed did not want their husbands to be more involved than they currently were. Some women did not want to give up control of the home domain; others did not want to share with their husbands the precious little time left with the children after the work day. Although not discussed in the literature, family support may be equally valid for men caring for disabled spouses or the elderly.

Institutional practices. The Select Committee on Families and Youth's hearing regarding the role of employed fathers concluded that societal attitude was the number one deterrent to greater father involvement in child tending (U.S. Congress, House of Representatives, 1991). When the breadwinner role is more valued than the caregiver role, it is difficult for men to modify their work role to take care of family members. Some men, though, are requesting workplace changes. DuPont's study of their employees found that over a five-year period men caught up with women on number of requests for flexible work options that would allow them to spend more time with their children (*Corporate News*, 1991).

Men's Experiences in the Caregiving Role

Comparative studies of male and female caregivers suggest that when men perform similar caregiving tasks for equal lengths of time, they report similar types of problems with their personal and work lives to those women cite (Burden & Googins, 1987; Fernandez, 1990; Schulz and Williamson, 1991).

Employed men and women, however, show differences in use of workplace and community resources. Although employed fathers often use short-term, informal leaves, they are less likely to take formal leaves from work to care for their children than are employed mothers.

Because of their concern about being perceived by co-workers and employers as effeminate and unmotivated workers, fathers' accommodations to the workplace are often invisible. According to James Levine (Director, Fatherhood Project, Families & Work Institute, N.Y.), they employ the following strategies: They wait for the boss to leave first and then they leave immediately afterwards; they tell co-workers they are going to another meeting when in fact they are leaving work to take care of their children; and finally, they try to be "Super Dads" by rising early and keeping hectic schedules (U.S. Congress, House of Representatives, 1991).

Kaye and Applegate (1990) found that employed caregivers to wives with Alzheimers' disease were ambivalent about respite care. They preferred services that were provided in their own home. This arrangement gave them more control by allowing them to watch over the home care providers. Policymakers at the workplace and government levels need to be aware of these special needs and concerns of employed male caregivers.

Effect of Active Fathering on Mothers and Children

Several research studies have indicated that children whose fathers were actively involved in their care and who established warm and close relationships were better adjusted as adults than those children who had the opposite experience (Lamb, 1987). Lamb qualifies this conclusion by stating that the father's caregiving activity needs to be perceived by all family members (including the father) as appropriate, wanted, and helpful.

A representative study of employed parents with a newborn infant found a positive relationship between husband's supportiveness and the employed mother's sense of well-being. Supportiveness was measured by amount of household help and infant care given, level of understanding of wife's job demands, degree of willingness to take time off or to help out when things got tough, and mother's perception of marital strain due to employment. The fathers' level of involvement in housework and child tending was low and consistent with other studies previously reported. Nonetheless, whatever assistance mothers did receive did matter (Gray, Lovejoy, Piotrkowski, & Bond, 1990).

SINGLE MOTHERS

Chante, a low-income single mother, told authorities she locked her daughter in her car trunk because she was unable to find a babysitter she could trust (Chicago Tribune, 1990). How many other single parents have struggled with finding affordable, high-quality child care?

Although employed single female parents are a heterogeneous group, with some enjoying the benefits of advanced education, moderate to high incomes, and high self-esteem, most single parents, like Chante, have multiple day-to-day pressures. Many single parents are disadvantaged by their limited education, low incomes, and inadequate child care. For the most part, employed single parents are a vulnerable group.

According to the Census Bureau, the number of single parents has almost tripled since 1970—going from 3.8 million to 9.7 in 1990. And their numbers are expected to increase in the coming years (U.S. Bureau of the Census, 1991). Like Chante, most single parents are female and many are employed fulltime (U.S. Department of Labor, 1991). The next section reviews the stressors experienced by employed single female parents.

Stressors and Their Consequences

Income and employment conditions. By far, the greatest difficulty faced by employed single female parents is economic. In 1991, the average yearly salary for single mothers was slightly over $15,000—$6,000 less than employed single fathers and $19,000 less than married parents with one earner

(U.S. Department of Labor, 1991). Their low wages place many single mothers in the category of the "working poor."

These low paying jobs often require single mothers to work irregular hours, such as weekends, nights, and rotating shifts (Hofferth, 1992). In many cases, the jobs held are of short duration or parttime and workers must keep looking for employment (Hofferth, 1992). Working conditions in low-paying jobs frequently have limited flexibility in work hours and limited access to telephones (Shinn, Ortiz-Torres, Morris, Simko, & Wong, 1987). Most employed single mothers have no health insurance and limited child care assistance from either workplaces or government (Hofferth, 1992).

Thus, even though single parents work, they have few resources. This in turn can increase their difficulty in managing work and family responsibilities.

Level of quality of child care. Irregular hours and low incomes make it very difficult for working single parents to get quality child care (Hofferth, 1992). Single parents are far more likely to rely on multiple child care arrangements, which often include reliance on relatives. Informal arrangements such as relative care have been found to break down more frequently than formal, outside-the-home arrangements (Hofferth et al., 1991).

Family day care or center-based services, often preferred to the more tenuous relative care, is too costly for single parents unless government or workplace subsidies are in place. This is unfortunate, because high-quality child care services have been found to improve cognitive and behavioral functioning of low-income children (Children's Defense Fund, 1992). It is not surprising that low-income single parents report less satisfaction with their child care arrangements than do upper-income mothers (Zaslow, Moore, & Zill, 1992).

Single parents spend a lot of money for their less-than-satisfactory child care. The Children's Defense Fund (1992) estimates that low-income families spend 27% of their income on child care compared to 6% for upper-income families. Like other parents, single parents want high-quality child care, but limited incomes and other employment-related limitations make it difficult for them to reach this goal.

Unstable child care arrangements affect the workplace. The *National Child Care Survey* found that 10% of women earning under $10,000 missed a day of work in the last month due to a child care failure compared to only 4% to 7% in all other income groups (Hofferth et al., 1991). In a three-company study, single female parents were absent more often than married female parents: 8.25 days compared to 7.22 days (Burden & Googins, 1987). Among low-income garment workers, 56% missed one or more weeks of work because of child care problems (Children's Defense Fund, 1992).

Because low-income workers generally have less flexible work schedules, they are more likely to lose a whole day of work when child care breaks down. These days often go unpaid, denying them a much needed income.

The day-to-day hassles and worries about children and the quality of the care they receive take their toll on single parents. Burden and Googins (1987) found that the more often parents had problems with child care arrangements, the more often they worried about their competency as parents and workers. As a result of this role strain, they felt more depressed and less satisfied with their jobs and with life in general (well-being). Shinn et al. (1987) also found that breakdowns in child care and related work absences increased single parents' number of perceived stressors and produced negative health and well-being outcomes.

Although single parents have reported more child care problems than other workers, they do not differ from other employed parents in job satisfaction or in their perception of job performance (Burden, 1988). They seem equally committed to their jobs and as fulfilled as other employees.

Characteristics of low-income single parents. In addition to limited resources, many low-income single parents have personal attributes that can contribute to their difficulties in managing work and family responsibilities. Low-income single parents are likely to be younger and less educated than employed parents in other income groups (Hofferth, 1992). They also tend to have more children than other income groups. Thirdly, they show higher depression levels, less effective coping responses, and less self-esteem than other employed parents (Hofferth, 1992; Shinn, Wong, Simko, & Ortiz-Torres, 1989). It is difficult to unravel personal qualities from life circumstances in terms of cause–effect relationships. It is clear, however, that the above characteristics, when present, can make it more difficult for single parents with limited incomes and few other resources to manage their enormous responsibilities.

Studies have found that children raised in homes with the environmental and maternal disadvantages just presented are more likely to have academic and behavioral problems, further compounding the stress on the parents (Zaslow et al., 1992).

ETHNIC CAREGIVERS

The population of the U.S. is becoming more ethnically and racially diverse; the proportion of whites decreased by 5% from 1960 to 1990, whereas blacks increased 2%, and other races (primarily Asians) grew 3%. By the year 2080, whites will make up only 72.6% of the entire population with nonwhites accounting for 27.4% (U.S. Bureau of the Census, 1989). Immigration accounts for about 25% of these population shifts (U.S. Bureau of the Census, 1992b).

Population changes affect the workplace. In 1985 only 17% of new hires came from nonnative whites; however by the year 2000, 42% of new entrants will be minorities (U.S. Department of Labor, 1987). These minority workers will have family responsibilities similar to if not exceeding those of their white co-workers. The next section looks at the experiences of minority working families in managing work and family tasks.

Stressors Faced by Minority Families

By all accounts, most minority families are disadvantaged. They have less disposable income, less adequate health insurance, fewer assets, and more family responsibilities than whites. In 1990, the average income of all white families with a member in the workforce was $36,000, for blacks it was

$24,327 and for Hispanics $26,288 (U.S. Department of Labor, 1991).

Asians, however, are an exception—they are more educated than other minority groups. Higher education generally leads to higher paying jobs and the benefits that go with them. Median income for Asians and Pacific Islanders in 1990 was $42,250. Their higher income is attributed, in part, to greater incidence of three or more earners per family. Of course, not all Asians fit this category (U.S. Bureau of the Census, 1992a). Some Asians and Pacific Islanders, such as Samoans and Vietnamese, have relatively low incomes. And a larger proportion of Asian and Pacific Islander than white families were below the poverty level in 1990 (U.S. Bureau of the Census, 1992a).

A major study by the National Center for Health Statistics found that persons with limited education and incomes had far more health problems and died sooner than those in higher socioecnomic groups. The study also noted that the gap between the health status of the affluent and the poor and minority groups had widened in the time period from 1960 to 1986 (Pappas, Queen, Hadden, & Fisher, 1993).

Almost twice as many blacks and Hispanics than whites were without health insurance in 1990 (U.S. Bureau of the Census, 1990b). Regarding family assets, 67% of whites owned their own home, while only 43% of blacks and 40% of Hispanics did so in 1990 (U.S. Bureau of the Census, 1990b).

Minorities are further disadvantaged by the degree of caregiving demands placed on them. One-parent family groups are three times more likely among black families and one-and-a-half times more likely among Hispanics than among white families (61%, 33%, 23%, respectively) (U.S. Bureau of the Census, 1990b). A black family is more likely to have a family member 15 years and over in need of assistance with everyday activities than whites or Hispanics (U.S. Bureau of the Census, 1990a). Thus, heavy caregiving demands continue throughout the family life cycle.

Another stressor experienced by some ethnic groups is isolation from the dominant society. Feelings of estrangement have many possible sources. For example, employed caregivers, not fluent in English, may find it very difficult to communicate their needs and to locate and obtain needed family care services. Employed immigrants, unaccustomed to nuances of American culture, may experience many communication problems as they try to negotiate service and other supports for their caregiving activities. Finally, conscious and unconscious acts of discrimination and prejudice by the dominant society can make it very difficult for minority groups to obtain the community and workplace assistance to which they are entitled.

Relationship between resources and family life. Limited resources can negatively affect the well-being of family members. For example, data from the *National Longitudinal Survey of Youth* found that minority mothers—particularly Hispanics—were more likely than other mothers to be unemployed because of their child care problems (Cattan, 1991). For employed blacks, the *National Child Care Survey* found that black children spent more time in child care than white or Hispanic children (Hofferth et al., 1991). The most likely reason, according to the researchers, was that black women were more likely to be single parents and for this reason had to work longer hours. When families can not find work when they need to, or have to work long hours, children are the losers.

The limited access to health care services experienced by most minority groups is a major contributor to their statistically poor health. Poor health can affect the ability of minority workers to hold down a job, raise a family, or take on other caregiving roles.

Work experiences of minority caregivers. Minority workers generally have jobs with low pay, inflexible hours, rigid routines, and less autonomy than jobs held by nonminorities. In a small study of employed black women, Katz and Piotrkowski (1983) found that lessened job autonomy and greater work demands were correlated with high role strain. Neal, Chapman, Ingersoll-Dayton, and Emlen (1993) found that the greater number of absences of minority employed caregivers were related to their less flexible work hours, which required missing the whole work day rather than a portion of the day.

In one study of employed caregivers to the elderly, black caregivers reported less support from their supervisors and less flexible policies regarding family concerns than white caregivers (Lechner, 1993). Similarly, employed mothers in Marlow's (1990) comparative study of Mexican-American and Anglo-American women found that Mexican-American women had less flexible work hours and less generous maternity leave policies than their white counterparts.

Although minority caregivers have fewer economic and workplace supports than white caregivers, they do not report greater stress in managing their work and caregiving roles. In the Neal et al. (1993) and the Lechner (1993) studies, there was no difference in the degree of stress experienced by the employed minority and nonminority caregivers. This is a curious result and may be explained, in part, by ethnic or racial differences in expectations and perceptions of the caregiving roles. Difference in the degree of family support for the caregiving role may also be a contributing factor. These issues are discussed next.

Minorities' Experience of the Caregiving Role

Regarding the care of children and working mothers, Fernandez's longitudinal studies of employed caregivers found that black and Hispanic mothers were less troubled by child care problems than white or Native American Indian mothers (1990). Fernandez suggests that because black women have a long history of managing work and family demands with few resources, they have learned effective ways to handle child care problems. Another stress reducing factor is black men's greater acceptance of the work role of women.

Similar findings regarding stress levels are present in studies of caregivers to the elderly. Blacks report lower perceived burden and less depression than white caregivers of the elderly (Lawton, Rajagopal, Brody, & Klebar, 1992; Morycz, 1985; Morycz, Malloy, Bozich, & Martz, 1987; Mui, 1992). The researchers surmised that black caregivers as compared to white caregivers were more accustomed to managing multiple role demands, more accepting of the caregiving experience, and less burdened by the day-to-day demands of caregiving.

Support from family and friends. Data from various studies suggest that minority families more frequently rely on and receive assistance from relatives. In the *National Child Care Survey* Hispanic and black children with employed parents were more likely to be cared for by relatives: whites—19%, blacks—42%, and Hispanics—31% (Hofferth et al., 1991). Although, as discussed earlier, relative care is less stable than center-based care, the willingness of relatives to help out is an important part of the experiences of minority families with young children.

Evidence suggests that caregiving commitment occurs throughout the life cycle. Employed black adult daughters of the elderly in the Lechner study (1993) indicated that their parents provided more emotional support and practical help to them as they were growing up than did the white daughters. As with child care assistance, black families were more available to their children than white families. It appears that for black families, caregiving is an integral part of the family's life experience from childhood to old age.

Although the literature highlights strong commitments to family caregiving among ethnic families, ethnic groups are not homogeneous and differences exist. Additionally, many factors unexplored in the literature can influence sustained caregiving commitments: socioeconomic level, the socialization process, level of acculturation, number of children, and many others (Lockery, 1991).

Policymakers at the workplace and government levels who are interested in reaching out to employed minority caregivers need to be cognizant of the varied experiences and needs of the growing number of ethnic workers with family responsibilities.

GAY AND LESBIAN CAREGIVERS

Demographic information about the gay population is very scanty. The Census Bureau does not ask questions on sexual identity. Researchers in the field of homosexuality think that 4% of adult men and 2% of adult women are gay ("The gay science," 1992).

The number of lesbian mothers is estimated to be from one to five million and gay fathers, one to three million (Patterson, 1992). A large proportion of these parents work. The number of homosexuals who care for aging parents is unknown.

Several factors are at work that may increase the number of gays who take on caregiving roles in the future. First, a review of major research studies concluded that children growing up in gay and lesbian households are not psychologically or socially damaged (Patterson, 1992). Second, recent studies of the brain suggest that homosexuality is biologically determined, not a personal or social choice (Bailey, Pillard, Neale, & Agyei, 1993). This finding may lead to greater tolerance of gays and lesbians. Third, workplace and public policies are beginning to recognize the legitimacy of gay and lesbian families. Greater understanding and tolerance among the heterosexual community may make it easier for gay men and lesbians to opt for raising a family.

Workplace Responses to Gay and Lesbian Caregivers

Unfortunately, there are no known studies of the experiences of employed gay and lesbian caregivers. Gays and lesbians are very fearful of persecution by employers and communities if they admit they are homosexual. For this reason it is very difficult to survey these groups.

In spite of lack of data on employed homosexual caregivers, a few workplace changes have been initiated that are relevant to them. In New York City, the Mayor granted individuals living together the right to register as "domestic partners." Registered gay and lesbian domestic partners who work for the city will be entitled to an unpaid leave to care for a new child (Finder, 1993). About 25 other cities and counties in the United States have this arrangement or some form of parental leave and/or medical benefit for domestic partners of government workers. Cities have taken the lead in offering nontraditional benefits, in part due to pressure from gay and lesbian advocacy groups. "It is easier for these groups to pressure a government into doing something because they are the public servants than to pressure private employers" (Bureau of National Affairs, 1991, p. 20).

A few workplaces have implemented leave programs and, to a lesser extent, health coverage for gay and lesbian couples. Health insurance coverage is far less likely because of cost concerns. The corporate list includes, but is not limited to, Time Inc., the *Village Voice*, Ben and Jerry's, Levi Strauss, Montefiore Hospital, and two leading universities (Bureau of National Affairs, 1991; De Palma, 1992; U.S. Congress, House of Representatives, 1991).

Unions have won leave and health benefits for nontraditional family members, including gay and lesbian couples. The first contract to include such clauses was negotiated in 1981 between the *Village Voice* and UAW Local 65 in New York City (Bureau of National Affairs, 1991).

These workplace, union, and government changes are small, but they indicate a growing trend toward helping gay and lesbian families manage their work and family responsibilities.

LONG-DISTANCE CAREGIVERS

What is it like to care for elderly relatives a long distance away? Not much is known about this experience, even though 18% of the U.S. work force who care for persons 50 years and over live more than an hour away from the elder (Galinsky, Bond & Friedman, 1993).

Research findings suggest that remote caregivers provide less assistance to their loved ones and perhaps as a consequence, experience less strain than those who live with or close to frail relatives (Horowitz, 1985; Kemper, 1992; Neal et al., 1993). The Bureau of National Affairs (1989) found that long-distance caregivers experienced a range of problems: psychological, financial, and organizational (i.e., coordination of agency services). Living far away increases the caregiver's worries about the relative's general condition, his or her acceptance of the care plan, the quality of the care provided, and arrangements to take time off from work. Financial costs can be extensive when travel time and loss of work time is taken into consideration. The long-distance caregiver is generally unaware of the services available in the relative's community. This makes setting up arrangements very difficult.

Geriatric Care Management

One of the services available to long-distance caregivers is geriatric care management which is generally located in communities with high concentrations of elderly persons. A care manager, as defined by the National Association of Private Geriatric Care Managers, is a "professional with a graduate degree in the field of human services or a substantial equivalent, certified or licensed at the independent practice level of his or her state or profession, who is duly trained and experienced in the assessment, coordination, monitoring, and direct delivery of services to the elderly and their families" (Bartelstone, 1993, p. 14). They act as an extension of the family and keep in contact with the faraway relative so that when adult children visit their parents they have time to socialize. The professional frees them from trying to arrange and take care of their parent's health needs in the short visit (Bartelstone, 1993).

Geriatric care management can be expensive, averaging from $60 to $150 dollars an hour. However, when the cost of travel and loss of job time is taken into consideration the fees may be affordable for many families. Some not-for-profit agencies such as Catholic Charities and Jewish Family and Children Services charge on a sliding scale (Bartelstone, 1993).

Competency levels of geriatric care managers and the range of services they provide can vary considerably from community to community. To help concerned relatives select qualified persons, Rona Bartelstone, an early pioneer in this field and past president of the National Association of Private Geriatric Care Managers, has developed a list of questions for prospective users to consider (Bartelstone,1993, p. 30). They include:

- What is the manager's educational experience with older adults and families?
- How long has the manager been in business? Is this a fulltime or parttime job?
- What licenses does the manager hold that permit functioning at the independent practice level?

- What are the manager's hours and availability during crises?
- In a one-person practice, how does the manager provide backup or coverage during illness or vacation?
- In a large practice, what are the staff's professions and qualifications? Do they work under supervision?
- What are the fees for services?
- What services does the manager provide directly? Which are arranged through outside providers? What is the manager's role once a referral is made?
- How does the manager keep the distant family informed?

Workplace Services

Caregivers to the elderly, as reported in Chapter 2, frequently need help locating suitable resources for their frail relatives. Resource and referral (R&R) services are highly desired by long-distance caregivers, but these services are not easy to provide.

Wagner and Hunt (1992) found in a study of users and nonusers of workplace elder care programs (counseling and R&R services) that nearly one half of the users were caring for relatives that lived outside the local area.

A study of R&R services provided by Partnership for Eldercare for five organizations in New York City investigated employee, employer, and agency responses to this service (Garrison & Jelin, 1990). This study found that a) long-distance caregivers frequently utilized this R&R service (22% of caregivers and 32% of pre-caregivers); b) locating out-of-state services was often complex, time consuming, and costly for the agency; c) unresolved long-distance assistance contributed to employee dissatisfaction with the service; and d) employers wanted enhanced capability for services to long-distance caregivers. The Partnership For Eldercare study found that long-distance R&R was not easy to provide because laws, eligibility requirements, number, type, and quality of health and social services for the aged vary enormously throughout the United States. Agencies wishing to implement or enhance services to long-distance caregivers need to consider findings from this study.

In addition to geriatric care management and R&R services, workplace programs such as lunch time seminars, handbooks, and support groups can help long-distance caregivers develop effective care strategies. Also other family members, in closer proximity to the elder, may be able to help or "spell" the working caregiver.

REFERENCES

Bailey, J. M., Pillard, R. C., Neale, M. C., & Agyei, Y. (1993). Heritable factors influence sexual orientation in women. *Archives General Psychiatry, 50*, 217–223.

Bartelstone, R. (1993, March–April). A solution for long distance care. *ANSWERS*, 13–15, 30.

Burden, D. S., & Googins, B. (1987). *Boston University: Balancing job and homelife study*. MA: Boston University School of Social Work.

Burden, D. S. (1988). Single parents and the work setting: The impact of multiple job and home life responsibilities. In F. E. Winfield (Ed.), *The work and family sourcebook* (pp. 479–490). Greenvale, NY: Panel Publishers.

Bureau of National Affairs. (1989). *Long distance eldercare: Spanning the miles with a new benefit* (Report No. 22). Washington, DC: Author.

Bureau of National Affairs. (1991). *Recognizing non-traditional families* (Report No. 38). Washington, DC: Author.

Cattan, P. (1991). Child-care problems: An obstacle to work. *Monthly Labor Review, 114*(10), 3–9.

Chicago Tribune. (1990, October 28). Mom who left girl in trunk may regain custody, p. 18.

Children's Defense Fund. (1992). *Child care: Key facts*. Washington, DC: Author.

Corporate News. (1991, April 17). Wilmington, DL: DuPont External Affairs.

De Palma, A. (1992, December 24). Benefits granted to gay partners. New York: *New York Times* (National), p. A13.

Fernandez, J. P. (1990). *The politics and reality of family care in corporate America*. Lexington, MA.: Lexington Books.

Finder, A. (1993, January 8). Rights of 'domestic partners' broadened by Dinkin's order. New York: *New York Times* (Metro), p. A1.

Galinsky, E., Bond, J. T., & Friedman, D. E. (1993). *Highlights: The National Study of the Changing Workforce*. New York: Families and Work Institute.

Garrison, A., & Jelin, M. A. (1990). *Partnership for eldercare research study*. New York: The New York City Department for the Aging.

The gay science of genes and brains. (1992, December 5). *The Economist*, 87–88.

Gray, E. B., Lovejoy, M. C., Piotrkowski, C. S., & Bond, J. T. (1990). Husband supportiveness and the well-being of employed mothers of infants. *Families in Society: The Journal of Contemporary Human Services*, 71, 332–341.

Hochschild, A. (1989). *Second shift*. New York: Viking Penguin.

Hofferth, S. L. (1992). *At the margin: Managing work and family life at the poverty line*. Presented at the Annual Meeting of the American Sociological Association, Pittsburgh, PA.

Hofferth, S. L., Brayfield, A., Deich, S., & Holcomb, P. (1991). *National child care survey, 1990*. Washington, DC: The Urban Institute Press.

Horowitz, A. (1985). Family caregiving to the frail elderly. In M. P. Lawton & G. L. Maddox (Eds.), *Annual review of gerontology and geriatrics Vol. 5* (pp. 194–246). New York: Springer.

Katz, M. H., & Piotrkowski, C. H. (1983). Correlates of family role strain among employed black women. *Family Relations*, *32*, 331–339.

Kaye, L. W., & Applegate, J. S. (1990). *Men as caregivers to the elderly*. Lexington, MA: Lexington Books.

Kemper, P. (1992). The use of formal and informal care by the disabled elderly. *Health Services Research*, *27*(4), 421–451.

Lamb, M. E. (1987). Introduction: The emergent father. In M. E. Lamb (Ed.), *The father's role: Cross cultural perspectives* (pp. 3–25). NJ: Erlbaum.

Lawton, P. M., Rajagopal, D., Brody, E., & Klebar, M. H. (1992). The dynamics of caregiving for a demented elder among black and white families. *Journal of Gerontology*, *47*, S156–S164.

Lechner, V. M. (1993). Racial group responses to work and parent care. *Families in Society: The Journal of Contemporary Human Services*, *74*, 93–103.

Lockery, S. A. (1991). Family and social supports: Caregiving among racial & ethnic minority elders. *Generations*, *15*(4), 58–62.

Marlow, C. (1990). Management of family and employment responsibilities by Mexican American women. *Social Work, 35*, 259–265.

Morycz, R. K. (1985). Caregiving strain and the desire to institutionalize family members with Alzheimer's disease. *Research on Aging, 7,* 329–357.

Morycz, R. K., Malloy, J., Bozich, M., & Martz, P. (1987). Racial differences in family burden: Clinical implications for social work. *Journal of Gerontological Social Work, 10,* 133–154.

Mui, A. C. (1992). Caregiver strain among black and white daughter caregivers: A role theory perspective. *The Gerontologist, 32,* 203–212.

Neal, M. B., Chapman, N. J., Ingersoll-Dayton, B., & Emlen, A. C. (1993). *Balancing work and caregiving for children, adults, and elders.* Newbury Park, CA: Sage.

Pappas, G., Queen, S., Hadden, W., & Fisher, G. (1993). The increasing disparity in mortality between socioeconomic groups in the United States, 1960 and 1986. *The New England Journal of Medicine, 329,* 103–109.

Patterson, C. J. (1992). Children of lesbian and gay parents. *Child Development, 63,* 1025–1042.

Pleck, J. H. (1989). *Family supportive employer policies and men's participation.* Paper prepared for the Panel on Employer's Policies and Working Families, Committee on Women's Employment and Related Social Issues, Commission on Behavioral and Social Sciences and Education, National Research Council, Washington, DC.

Pleck, J. H. (1993). Are "family-supportive" policies relevant to men? In J. C. Hood (Ed.), *Work, families and masculinities.* Newbury Park, CA: Sage.

Schulz, R., & Williamson, G. M. (1991). A 2–year longitudinal study of depression among Alzheimer's caregivers. *Psychology and Aging, 6,* 569–578.

Shinn, M., Wong, N. W., Simko, P. A., & Ortiz-Torres, B. (1989). Promoting the well-being of working parents: Coping, social support, and flexible job schedules. *American Journal of Community Psychology, 17,* 31–55.

Shinn, M., Ortiz-Torres, B., Morris, A., Simko, P. A., & Wong, N. W. (1987). *Child care patterns, stress, and job behaviors among working parents.* Presented at 95th Annual Convention of the American Psychological Association, New York.

U.S. Bureau of the Census. (1989). *Projections of the population of the United States by age, sex, and race: 1988 to 2080* (Current Population Reports, Series P-25, No. 1018). Washington, DC: U.S. Government Printing Office.

U.S. Bureau of the Census. (1990a, June). *The need for personal assistance with everyday activities: Recipients and caregivers* (Current Population Reports, Series P-70, No. 19). Washington, DC: U.S. Government Printing Office.

U.S. Bureau of the Census. (1990b, December). *How we're changing: Demographic state of the nation* (Current Population Reports, Series P-23, No. 170). Washington, DC: U.S. Government Printing Office.

U.S. Bureau of the Census. (1991). *Population profile of the United States 1991* (Current Population Reports, Series P-23, No. 173). Washington, DC: U.S. Government Printing Office.

U.S. Bureau of the Census. (1992a). *The Asian and Pacific Islander population in the United States March 1991 and 1990* (Current Population Reports, Series P-20, No. 459). Washington, DC: U.S. Government Printing Office.

U.S. Bureau of the Census. (1992b). *Population trends in the 1980s* (Current Population Reports, Series P-23, No. 175). Washington, DC: U.S. Government Printing Office.

U.S. Department of Labor. (1987). *Workforce 2000: Work and Workers for the 21st Century.* Washington, DC: Hudson Institute.

U.S. Department of Labor, Bureau of Labor Statistics. (1991, January). *Employment and Earnings.* Washington, DC: U.S. Government Printing Office.

U.S. Congress, House of Representatives. (1991, June 11). *Babies and brief cases: Creating a family-friendly workplace for fathers* (Select Committee on Children, Youth, and Families, 102nd Congress. Pub. No. 45–219). Washington, DC: Government Printing Office.

Wagner, D. L., & Hunt, G. G. (1992). *Factors influencing utilization of workplace programs by employed caregivers.* Paper presented at 45th Annual Scientific Meeting of the Gerontological Society of America, Washington, DC.

Zaslow, M., Moore, K., & Zill, N. (1992, January). *Implications of the JOBS program for children.* Draft paper prepared for The Urban Institute, Washington, DC.

4 Employee Benefits

Almost half of the U.S. work force have some type of dependent care responsibility. This chapter takes a look at how work organizations and government are responding to the needs of employed caregivers. The following sections are included: background information, rising corporate response, role of government in dependent care, employee benefits and services, and future trends.

BACKGROUND INFORMATION

Definition of Benefits

Benefits can be defined as nonsalary compensation by the employer to the employee (Saltford and Heck, 1990). Employee benefits have become, over the years, a major component of the compensation offered to workers by American companies. They include both direct fringe benefits such as health insurance, annual and sick leave, holidays, and retirement plans, and indirect ones such as the employer's share of social security taxes (U.S. Merit Systems Protection Board, 1991). The U.S. Chamber of Commerce estimated that voluntary corporate contributions to benefits by employers in 1986 represented 30.4% of wages and salaries, while another 8.9% was contributed for legally required benefits (U.S. Chamber of Commerce, 1986).

Historical Perspectives

For some 200 years nonsalary compensation has consistently developed in the direction of a wider array of programs. In recent years, employers have been offering more choices to the worker while attempting to hold the line on costs to the company. Employee benefit programs date to colonial times. Galatin Glassworks inaugurated the first profit-sharing plan in 1797. The first corporate pension plan was established in 1875 by American Express, some years after the New York City Police Department plan. Montgomery Ward offered the first group health plan for employees in 1910 (Hewitt Associates, 1991).

Saltford and Heck (1990) note three broad phases in the development of benefits in the 20th century. In the 1940s and 1950s, pensions and other benefits were negotiated by unions and subsequently extended to other groups. Here one may add that the World War II period, with its controls on salaries, resulted in a growing emphasis on nonsalary benefits. In the 1960s and 1970s there was an expansion of benefits and broadened coverage, which moderated somewhat in the 80s. Finally in the third phase, the 90s, a focus has developed on greater flexibility, with greater emphasis on employee choice among benefits. William J. Wiatrowski (1990) also suggests that there have been three stages in benefits development in the past 75 years—first a period in which employers provided no benefits, second a stage offering a standard package of benefits designed for a male-supported family, and third, the provision of innovative and flexible benefits to meet differing family needs.

Mandated and voluntary benefits. One must begin with the federally mandated Social Security program initiated in 1935 and the Medicare program instituted in 1965 because of their sheer importance in America. Other mandatory benefits include contributions to federal and state unemployment insurance taxes and contributions to federal, state, local, and private sector workers' compensation funds.

Voluntary benefits, that is, benefits not mandated by law, include life insurance, health insurance, retirement plans, and long-term disability insurance. Vacation and sick leave are commonly offered. But family supports such as parental leave, child care, and elder care are still far less common (Saltford & Heck, 1990).

Health care has been a primary component in the development of benefits. In 1950 less than 50% of the civilian labor force had this coverage, but by 1970 80% were covered and workplace coverage had become the primary means of insurance in America. As has been widely reported in the media, corporations are increasingly worried about the costs of health care and various methods are being attempted in an effort to control the rapid growth of such costs. Kolodrubetz (1972) noted that health care grew from 20% of benefit costs in 1950 to more than 40% by 1970. The *EBRI Databook on Employee Benefits* notes that employer spending for health insurance (excluding Medicare) increased an average of 15.3% a year from 1948 to 1988, rising to a total of $133 billion in 1988 (Employee Benefits Research Institute, 1991).

Cost sharing, preferred providers, and other health benefit cost management efforts are underway today (Employee Benefits Research Institute, 1991). Undoubtedly the struggle to control health benefit costs will powerfully affect the development of other benefits as we approach the 21st century. Likewise, the prospect of continuing rises in social security taxes will affect increases in, or even the availability of, other nonsalary forms of compensation. On the other hand, limitations on high-cost benefits may be accompanied by an increasing array of relatively low-cost benefits, such as dependent care, which identify the employer's concern about employee issues.

The increasing role of women in the work force. The work force needs of employers have greatly affected the development of benefits. For example, there was a tremendous surge in the availability of child care during World War II, when there was a great need for women in the workplace. The Lanham Acts of 1940 and 1941 provided for community-based child care programs in defense plant areas. However the appropriations to support such programs ceased after the war. As soon as the war related demand for women workers subsided, there was a major drop in the availability of child care. Despite the loss of these programs, the proportion of women in the work force with children under age six increased from 11% in 1948 to 24% in 1966 (Magid, 1983).

In recent years the women's movement, and, perhaps more importantly, the falling birthrate and the needs of the economy have contributed to a significant increase in the number of women in the U.S. work force. As noted in Chapter 1, by 1990, 74% of all women with children between the ages of 6 and 17%, and 53% of those with children under one year of age were in the labor force (U.S. Bureau of the Census, 1992). Thus, the decades since World War II have seen a steady rise in the proportion of all women, and particularly those with families, in the work force outside the home.

THE RISING CORPORATE RESPONSE

Rodgers and Rodgers (1989) cite four reasons for what they regard as rapid growth in corporate interest in work–family programs: (1) Work force demographics are changing, (2) employee perceptions are changing, (3) evidence is increasing that inflexibility has an adverse impact on productivity, and (4) concern about America's children is growing fast.

The growing participation of mothers in the work force is complemented by the rising awareness that men have family responsibilities. Indeed, *Across the Board*, a publication of the Conference Board (a corporate thinktank) published an article on "Fathers and the Corporation" in March, 1986. In the article, James Levine cites corporate ads addressed to working fathers. He notes that five or ten years previously "The idea that dad might need to hurry home, or might feel a conflict between his commitments to work and family, would not have been aired" (p. 8). John Fernandez, in his recent book, *The Politics and Reality of Family Care in Corporate America* (1990), observes also that the biggest change between studies he conducted in 1984 and 1988 was the significantly higher percentage of men who had at least some child care problem in 1988.

Our expanding consciousness of work–family concerns is also illustrated by Keitel's 1980 review of quality of working-life initiatives prior to 1980 for the U.S. Office of Personnel Management. There was no mention of such topics as day care or elder care or work at home, and flexible work arrangements were mentioned only briefly (Keitel, 1980). Yet already in 1980 the Catalyst Center surveyed the CEO's of the *Fortune* 1300 companies and found that corporations were concerned about the phenomenon of two-career families because it could affect recruitment, employee morale, and productivity. Seventy-three percent of the respondents also said that they favored flexible work hours, although only 37% had them (Catalyst Career and Family Center, 1981).

In the early 80s Magid (1983) found in a survey of 204 companies regarding child care initiatives that work site child care centers were the most common initiative but alternative work schedules in combination with working parent seminars or information and referral services in combination with child care vouchers were also becoming common. The benefits to the companies of such programs, as stated by executives, were: recruitment advantage, improved morale, lower absenteeism, less turnover, higher rates of return of persons on leave, and improved work satisfaction, along with a variety of other factors.

Workplace programs and policies responsive to elder care followed the development of child care initiatives. The demographic changes in American society reported in chapter one have provided the basis for these developments. The first survey of employees to focus on employee obligations for the care of elders was the Travelers Insurance Company internal survey of their employees in 1985. That survey found that some 20% had such caregiving duties (Travelers, 1987). Although the exact number of working caregivers is unknown, the likelihood is that elder care will affect a growing proportion of employees as the baby boom enters midlife and the older population expands. Thus Buck Consultants (1991) found in their survey of employers that 54% of them regarded elder care as a priority for the nineties, as opposed to only 6% in the eighties.

Stages of Workplace Responses

The Families and Work Institute (Galinsky, Friedman, & Hernandez, 1991) describe three stages in the evolution of work and family programs: In Stage 1 the companies develop a few inexpensive benefits such as a child care resource and referral service; in Stage 2 a top-level commitment to work–family issues emerges and they move from a piecemeal approach to an integrated one; in Stage 3 work and family programs become part of their overall business strategy. For example, companies such as Johnson and Johnson and DuPont have added specific statements about supporting the family obligations of their workers to their corporate credos. The Institute's survey of *Fortune* 500 companies revealed that more than three fourths of the companies surveyed had not passed Stage 1 (Galinsky et al., 1991).

Rodgers and Rodgers (1989) also note three broad areas of corporate response: first, dependent care; second, greater flexibility in hours, location and time of work, and career paths that allow for family responsibility; and third, formal company statements validating family issues coupled with manager training. They observe that few companies are active in all three and that many are active in none.

Extent of Workplace Benefits

Friedman (1991) states that there are some 5,400 companies in the U.S. offering child care initiatives for their employees, but Fernandez (1990) comments that "Most business executives . . . have not yet taken the step of assisting their employees" (p. xviii). Magid, in a review of the state of work–family programs asserts, "Much of corporate America has ignored the problems of employee caregivers, despite the frequent warnings over the last 10 years" (Magid, 1991, p. 7). Saltford and Heck (1990) note that few small businesses offer child care assistance. They cite Bureau of Labor statistics data which showed only 4% of medium and large companies subsidizing child care benefits in 1988.

The 1980s was a decade of rapid change in awareness

regarding work–family issues, starting with child care concerns and moving to elder care concerns. Perhaps the single most important advance in corporate policies in the last few years is the change from "child care policies" to either "work–family" or "dependent care policies" (Rodgers & Rodgers, 1989). This change allows for employees caring for the frail elderly or disabled children and adults to take advantage of leave and related arrangements, if such exist.

The continuing growth in the proportion of women in the work force, the growing number of elderly persons, the changing perspective on the impact of work on family, and vice versa, along with the leadership of some major corporations, has created an environment where human resource executives are more aware of the needs of their employees and of the recruitment and retention advantages accruing to companies which develop work–family programs. At the same time, there are many companies which have not begun to address work–family concerns today.

RECENT LEGISLATION CONCERNING DEPENDENT CARE

Government legislation affects the work and family domains through income distribution, family-related work leaves, health care financing, and child and elder care resources. Several public initiatives are reviewed here.

The Family and Medical Leave Act which President Clinton signed in 1993 requires businesses with 50 or more employees to grant a 12-week leave to employees caring for newborns, newly adopted children, and frail close relatives. Jobs are guaranteed and health benefits continue during the leave period, but wages are not guaranteed.

A growing number of states also have enacted legislation requiring employers to provide leave for varied periods of time in relation to child-birth, illness, or family emergency. Thirty-three states and the District of Columbia had either established or were pursuing parental or maternity leave policies in 1987–1988. Also relevant to the issue of family leave is the Pregnancy Discrimination Act of 1978 which requires states with disability insurance for employees to treat pregnancy as a disability. Thus, women living in states with this benefit are granted paid maternity/disability leaves (U.S. Department of Labor, 1989).

The child and dependent care tax credit enables those who qualify to deduct a portion of their dependent care expenses on their federal tax forms. On the state level, 29 states offer dependent care tax provisions, 21 have tax credits, and 8 have tax deductions (Creedon & Tiven, 1989). These tax credits primarily benefit moderate-income families. Assistance for low income families comes from the federal Child Care and Development Block Grant, passed in 1990. It helps low-income families pay for their child care services and helps states improve the quality and supply of child care services. (See also Chapter 8 on Public–Private Partnerships.)

The Economic Recovery Tax Act of 1981 (ERTA) provides tax incentives for employer-sponsored dependent care benefits. Dependent care assistance plans (DCAPs), qualified under IRS § 129, provide incentives for both employers and employees. Employers can deduct from income tax the cost of providing child care and elder care benefits. An employee can exclude from taxable income up to $5,000 annually contributed to a DCAP. Eligible expenses are limited to dependents under age 15 and elderly or disabled dependents. However, it should be noted also that the dependent must be living with the employee eight hours a day, the dependent must also be dependent for tax purposes, and the employee must be paying 51% of the costs of their care (Employee Benefit Research Institute, 1988).

As of 1989, some 29 states had enacted dependent care tax credits, and adult dependents were covered in 28 states. The availability of tax incentives for dependent care programs and for employee expenses related to care services is of great importance, and may be used by many for elder care service provision in the future. However, as currently written, the regulations make it very difficult to use DCAP programs for elder care purposes (Creedon, 1991).

The growth of federal and state legislation in the work–family area, especially in regard to leave-of-absence policies, will place great pressures on companies, particularly those with widely dispersed work locations, to implement leave policies on a national basis. Government at all levels employs an increasing share of the work force, and, as an employer, government has also responded to work–family issues. Thus, through both legislation and policy, government is a powerful force in defining benefits and programs relevant to work and family concerns.

EMPLOYEE BENEFITS AND SERVICES

Leave Policies and Flexible Work Schedules

The workplace programs most often available to help employees with family responsibilities are flexible time and leave policies. Time to take care of family problems is one of the most frequently cited elder care needs (Wagner, Creedon, Sasala, & Neal, 1989) and child care needs among employed caregivers (Fernandez, 1990). Where they are in place, flex policies and leaves are available to almost all employees, not just those with family responsibilities.

Flextime, flex-place and compressed work weeks. Although employees work a full week under a flex schedule, they have some choice in determining the start and end of the workday. All employees work "core" times in midmorning and mid-afternoon. Those who use flex cannot change their hours whenever they feel like it; they are expected to use a regular routine. Variations can include seasonal hours, compressed work weeks, and part-time employment.

The cost of such a benefit is low and easy to administer. Fernandez (1990) also notes that morale of employees increases, overall productivity improves, and commuting patterns are eased. Saltford and Heck (1990) also report that some studies show a decrease in tardiness and absenteeism associated with flextime. Such work flexibility can allow two-career families to juggle responsibilities for care more easily and can reduce leave time and staff turnover.

Of course there are some types of work which do not lend themselves to flextime (shift work springs to mind). Supervisors may not be present for some of the period and may therefore resist flextime use by an employee. Problems in arranging meetings may have to be overcome.

Several surveys of work and family options within primarily large corporations report that from 52% to 77% of these companies now offer flextime schedules (Bureau of National Affairs, 1991a; Galinsky et al., 1991; Hewitt Associates, 1990; International Foundation of Employee Benefit Plans, 1990). However, Saltford and Heck (1990) note that the trend toward flextime has slowed in recent years. They cite a 1985 Department of Labor study which found that only 12.3% of the labor force operates on some form of flextime.

Seasonal flex is easier to operate because it affects all employees. Summer hours programs typically offer employees longer weekends—which could help with caregiving chores.

Part-time employment is twice as prevalent among women than men, according to Saltford and Heck (1990). Some companies offer this option to all employees, others only to administrative and clerical employees (Bureau of National Affairs, 1991c). The Work and Families Institute survey of the *Fortune* 500 companies found that 87.8% of respondents offer such options (Galinsky et al., 1991). Some companies offer full benefits to employees who have to opt for part-time work. For others there can be a significant benefits loss.

Job sharing is another option which allows two employees to split a job. They must ensure that the total hours per week for that job are completed. The difficulties involved in developing such arrangements are acknowledged by many experts and it is unlikely to become a widely used option. Similarly, *home-based work* is becoming a more feasible option because of new technologies. However, since very few companies offer this option, it is primarily feasible for the self-employed. Yet home is expected to be the work site for up to 40 million workers by the year 2000 (Saltford & Heck, 1990).

Flextime, job sharing, part-time employment and compressed work weeks are likely to become the most common work–family related benefits by the year 2000, according to the International Foundation of Employee Benefit Plans survey of employers in 1989 (1990).

Leave policies. About 40% of all working women are eligible for a six-to-ten-week maternity leave benefit including partial wages and job guarantees (Kahn & Kamerman, 1987). This benefit is tied to disability insurance that is mandated in five states—California, New York, New Jersey, Hawaii, and Rhode Island. Most large corporations also offer a maternity leave, but wage replacements and job guarantees are not uniform (Galinsky et al., 1991; Hewitt Associates, 1990). Small companies are less likely to offer nonmandated maternity leaves (Buck Consultants, 1990). Small corporations cite cost and difficulty in temporarily replacing employees. However, a report commissioned by the Small Business Administration indicates that it is less costly to grant a six-week unpaid leave to an employee for childbirth, adoption, or serious family illness than to terminate the employee and hire a replacement (Bureau of National Affairs, 1991b).

With the passage of the Family and Medical Leave Act of 1993, employers with 50 or more employees are mandated to provide a 12-week unpaid leave for family emergencies, with continuing health and retirement benefits. Many companies, though, have had leave policies, whether formal or informal, for some time. Some companies base the amount of time allowed on years of service, and in some cases leave can last as long as a year. At Chevron, employees can take up to 6 months for care of a seriously ill family member while maintaining health coverage and continuing to accumulate credit toward retirement. They return to the same or a similar job. Nordstrom employees can take up to 12 weeks in any 2-year period; Honeywells Space Systems Group employees can take up to six months (Bureau of National Affairs, 1991c).

In a survey of state governments as employers conducted by the National Association of State Units on Aging and the International Personnel Management Association, the use of sick leave for caregiving was found to be widely available as official policy. The amount of sick leave that could be used ranged from 3 to 30 days (Creedon & Tiven, 1989). Employees always, of course, have been able to use annual vacation for child and elder care purposes and anecdotal evidence indicates that the use of sick leave for care purposes is also common.

Leave sharing has been pioneered by the federal government. In 1988 the Federal Leave Sharing Act was signed into law allowing federal employees to donate annual leave to another employee so that he or she does not lose income during an emergency. The second element of the law required the establishment of an 'insurance' type of arrangement where employees could set aside a minimum amount of their own leave in advance of any emergency in a "leave bank." Then, after exhausting their own leave sources they could request a grant from the bank. Employees experiencing a personal or family medical emergency can avail themselves of leave through the bank after they have exhausted their own annual leave and accumulated sick leave.

In its November 1991 report to the President and Congress, the U.S. Merit Systems Protection Board stated that over 22,000 employees had donated leave to co-workers. Over 8,000 workers had made use of the donated leave, using an average of four to five weeks of donated leave each. The report states that agencies are very happy with the leave transfer program, and its cost to the federal government should be very small since it is supported primarily by the generosity of employees. Restrictions on the amount and timing of donations minimize the possibility that employees will donate leave that they would have forfeited anyway (i.e., "use or lose" leave). Donors are prohibited from donating sick leave. (During a 1987 experimental period, sick leave could also be donated, but the Office of Personnel Management found that most workers offered sick leave days when the option was available, and this would result in a significant net cost to the government.) The "Balancing Work Responsibilities and Family Needs" report from the U.S. Merit Systems Protection Board (November, 1991) suggests that leave-transfer is a better approach than the leave bank idea. Reservations specified include the recognition that leave-transfer is a voluntary arrangement—it is only available if gifts are made. The board also notes that the government is offering a fringe benefit paid for by other employees, and this may not be the image the federal government wants to convey to its employees. However, on balance the board strongly endorses this successful program. Because of its success, the 1993 sunset on this Act has been removed because of its success (J. Seidman, Office of Personnel Management, personal communication, January 28, 1994).

Extended treatment has been provided to this federal program because it offers an example of an extremely successful collaboration between employer and employees to help employees with family emergencies. It may, therefore, be replicated by other employers. The Robert Wood Johnson Foundation has had a program for some time to foster Service-Credit banks at the workplace. Service Credits operate as a barter system, allowing an employee to provide physical assistance or expertise to another while receiving credits from a pool which can be redeemed at a later time for services needed by the emloyee or her/his family. The pooling of employee resources in such fashion may be a major trend of the future. The extensive *BNA's Directory of Work and Family Programs* (Bureau of National Affairs, 1991a) does not include a leave-sharing category, which suggests that the federal model is not yet widespread in industry. The Family and Medical Leave Act provides only unpaid leave, so leave-sharing and leave-bank concepts are very viable means of removing the loss-of-income barrier to use of leaves.

Resource and Referral

The most common benefit targeted to working caregivers is the resource and referral service (R&R) (Bureau of National Affairs, 1991a; Galinsky et al., 1991). In the Families and Work Institute survey, of some 188 respondents from the *Fortune* 500 companies, 54.5% offer child care R&R and 21% offer elder care consultation and referral to their employees (Galinsky et al., 1991). More than half of all employers surveyed by The International Foundation of Employee Benefit Plans in 1990 expect to offer elder care R&R services and 45% plan to offer child care R&R to their employees by the year 2000.

The resource and referral service is normally provided by an external contractor, though some companies offer it on an internal basis. The employee can call a dedicated line or 800 number, and obtain assistance in locating a suitable resource.

Child and elder care R&R services generally operate as separate services with unique 800 numbers.

Child care resource and referral. Employees who call the child care R&R number are usually given the names of three child care providers in their geographic area. Several R&R services also help employees decide what child care options are right for them (e.g., family care, child care center) and how to judge the quality of the care provided by the various providers. This service is very helpful to busy parents who are trying to locate the best possible and most affordable care arrangements among oftentimes limited choices. R&R services, with good management information systems, are able to supply community planners and local providers with employee preferences and service gaps. Some R&R services, in response to employee and community concerns about provider availability, cost, and quality, have assisted in recruiting and training providers within the local communities. IBM initiated the first nationwide corporate sponsored child care R&R in 1984. AT&T and others soon followed. These companies often contract with businesses that have the capacity to offer a nationwide comprehensive R&R service for child care.

Although IBM was the leader in the development of corporate R&R, many R&R services were initially developed with public initiatives and funds. For example, in the late 1970s, Governor Brown provided modest funding to launch several Child Care R&R offices in California. These R&R services were originally established to assist low income families with locating and paying for child care services (Kahn & Kamerman, 1987). The Human Services Reauthorization Act of 1984 allows federal block grant money to be used for state and local R&R agencies that offer dependent care information (Zigler & Lang, 1991). Many of these not-for-profit agencies have contracts with corporations.

Elder care consultation and referral. For elder care concerns, a professional counselor will help the employee assess the needs of the older relative and then provide advice as to appropriate resources to meet those needs. If the elder is at a distance from the employee or the service needs are complex, the service will carry out a search for the appropriate services in the elder's area and will call back within a specified period of time (usually within 48 hours unless it is an emergency) with names, addresses, and phone numbers for appropriate service agencies. The R&R person will make a follow-up call within a limited period of time to ensure that the connection to services has been made and that it is satisfactory.

Services such as those described above can be of great assistance to caregiver employees, especially in the early stages of dependent care. Often the onset of elder care is sudden, through a fall or stroke, and adult children may have no knowledge of the services available to help elders either near at hand or far away. The number one need of caregivers in many studies has been information (Scharlach, Lowe, & Schneider, 1991; Wagner et al., 1989). However, R&R service suffers from the handicap of being an "over the phone" response. Often the caregiver making the call is at a significant distance from the elderly relative and has a poor understanding of their needs. A further problem with R&R programs is that they cannot recommend services if none exist to meet the need (Rodgers & Rodgers, 1989). Finally, after information is received, the employee or the family must then take the responsibility for, and perhaps bear the cost of, the actual services provided to the elder.

Currently, a number of national organizations, both not-for-profit and profit, offer elder care R&R service to employers. In a number of communities, local service agencies or vendors offer this form of help to employers in the region. The first R&R service known to the authors for elder care was implemented by Hallmark in 1988. In 1989, IBM implemented a nationwide program, and a wide range of major companies have since established such service. The U.S. Social Security Administration began a pilot program in the Atlanta region in 1990.

Jack Hansen, in an editorial in *Aging Network News* in August, 1989, urged that corporate executives not reinvent the wheel in developing R&R services. He pointed out the fact that there is an information and referral service provided by each of the 670 Area Agencies on Aging throughout the nation.

That public service needs both technological and professional assistance, but he suggested that an alliance between the corporate and public sectors could enhance the capability of this existing national network and make it accessible to the work force at a much lower cost than that represented by a myriad of contracts with private vendors. The National Association of Area Agencies on Aging in collaboration with The National Association of State Units on Aging have implemented a national Eldercare Locator Hotline, access number (1-800-677-1116), so that one can find out the nearest Area Agency on Aging information and referral service for the location of an older relative.

Work and Family Seminars and Support Groups

Seminars, or brown bag lunches, have been offered at a wide variety of companies, as a first step in the company response to broad work–family issues. Some 25% of the respondents to the recent Families and Work Institute survey of the *Fortune* 500 companies offer work and family seminars (Galinsky et al., 1991). Although seminars dealing with child care concerns were offered first, the Travelers Insurance Company began offering programs on elder care immediately after its elder care survey was completed in 1985 (Bureau of National Affairs, 1988). Topics covered can include: infant and toddler care, raising adolescents, parenting for fathers, selecting and judging child care arrangements, the aging process, communication with older relatives, housing options for older relatives, wills and trusts, community services for the elderly, and a variety of other issues.

The general experience to date seems to be that lunch time is the optimum time to offer these programs, although there are obvious constraints of time attached to this. Some companies permit participants to take an extended lunch hour for program participation. The number of participants can range between twenty and more than one hundred, and the extent of advertising has a significant impact on participation. Females are much more likely to attend these programs, and outreach to male employees remains a challenge (Creedon, 1987).

Support groups have also been conducted at a number of companies, although to a lesser extent than educational seminars. The Families and Work Institute survey reports that only 5.3% of respondents offer this option (Galinsky et al., 1991). The Travelers has offered a professionally staffed support group for caregivers of elderly relatives continuously since 1986. Members are free to come and go, and those who participate have been heavily burdened caregivers (Bureau of National Affairs, 1991c). It may be worth noting that Dr. Margaret Neal found that females were the major participants in recent support groups in Oregon; males only participated in an after-hours program (Neal, 1992). This replicates findings from the University of Bridgeport project where males participated in only one support group, which was conducted after work hours (Creedon, 1987).

Lunch time seminars and support groups at the workplace can be offered by the Employee Assistance Program (EAP) or Health Promotion staff of the company. At relatively little cost, local expertise can be hired to conduct such programs also. These low-cost interventions can be very beneficial to a range of employees. Renee Magid (1991) suggests that an ongoing educational program, keyed by a continuing work–family educational series staffed by a professional, can be the backbone of a company response to its employee caregivers. Magid also emphasizes that quality is essential if employees are to make use of such programs and that this cannot be achieved without effort. At most companies these programs are offered free to employees. Merck, however, has offered Family Matter Workshops since 1985 for which employees pay a portion of the cost. Neal (1992) has also offered programs with a small fee to participants. She has found that charging a series fee produces a slight but positive influence on attendance at a larger number of sessions.

Employee Assistance Programs

Employee Assistance Programs (EAP) have had a mandate to deal with family issues in many corporations for some years. Surveys of large corporations report that from 49% to 86% of these firms offer an Employee Assistance Program (Hewitt Associates, 1990; Galinsky et al., 1991; International Foundation of Employee Benefit Plans, 1990). According to the Families and Work Institute survey (Galinsky et al., 1991), 6% of the U.S. work force annually utilize the EAP.

The scope of EAP assistance is as broad as one's definition of 'problems of living', and confidential one-on-one counseling is the core service. The EAP staffer can assess the problem; offer short-term counseling; make referrals to child, adult, and elder care resources; and follow up with referrals to outside resources if longer term help is needed. Besides counseling, EAPs have developed support groups, caregiver fairs, seminars on a range of topics, and information and referral services. The EAP is therefore a logical internal resource for dealing with child, dependent adult, and elder care concerns. Indeed, Sarah Mullady, corporate director of EAPs for Champion International, suggests that AIDS, caring for elderly dependents, and alcoholism will be the issues presenting the greatest challenges to employers in the 90s, and EAPs will be on the frontline of corporate responses to them (Bureau of National Affairs, 1988).

While the EAP is potentially a major resource for workplace response to elder care concerns, in many cases the professional staff have little or no expertise in this area. Kevin Gorey and his colleagues, in a survey of EAPs in New York State, found that more than 90% of respondents claimed no expertise on elder care (Gorey, Brice, & Rice, 1990). Because the company has an EAP, it may claim to offer support for family problems, including elder care. However, if there is no additional staff allocation and no specific training on the subject, one may be skeptical about the level of effective responsiveness to elder care.

The good news is that companies can require their contract EAP (and 50% of EAP programs are carried out by an outside vendor) to provide appropriate expertise as a part of the contract. Also, Gorey, Brice, and Rice (1990) have demonstrated that a 2-day intensive training can provide a solid minimum knowledge base for corporate EAP staff, ensuring that there is at least a basic capability to respond to elder care problems. This should not represent a major cost for the employer. Similar training for child and dependent adult care may be equally necessary.

The EAP has the potential to serve not only the individual employee but also the entire family. At least some companies now offer family consultation as a part of the response to elder care. This can help greatly in gaining the involvement of the larger family system and thus reducing the stress on the employee caregiver.

Child Care Services

As mentioned in Chapter 2, one of the greatest concerns of working parents is the quality of the care their children receive while they are at work. Likewise, child care experts express much concern about the social and cognitive development of children who do not receive adequate care during their formative years. They believe that these children are ill prepared to be productive members of society.

Prior to the influx of women into the work force, female relatives and neighbors were available to care for children of working parents. These babysitters have been replaced by a network of child care providers, including in-home care, family day care, and child care centers.

In an effort to help working parents obtain affordable and quality child care services, some work organizations provide some type of child care assistance to their employed parents. Surveys of child care initiatives in the workplace indicate that from 5% to 13% of the companies surveyed sponsor child care centers on or near the worksite for their employees and 3% to 12% offer financial assistance, including vouchers and child care discounts (Galinsky et al., 1991; Hewitt, 1990; International Foundation of Employee Benefit Plans, 1990).

Although some companies build and operate their own child care centers, this is not the common arrangement. Most companies provide space for the child care program and turn operations over to a profit or not-for-profit child care service (Zigler & Lang, 1991). The cost to the parents for the child care service is generally reduced. Employed parents with small children, who easily can be transported to the center, are very pleased with this type of company benefit. This arrangement, though, is less feasible for parents with school-aged children.

In an effort to share costs, several companies may join together to sponsor a child care consortium at a location near each company's work site. Because of the high costs to the employer of single employer or consortia child care programs, it is unlikely that this benefit will grow much in the near future.

Vouchers and discounts issued by the employer, as well as dependent care assistance plans (DCAPs, discussed earlier), can reduce the employee's child care costs for community-based centers of the employee's choosing. Financial assistance programs are easier for companies to administer than child care centers and they are less costly. For these reasons this benefit is expected to increase in the future.

A third way in which companies have participated in child care initiatives is through direct involvement with community-based child care settings. For example, AT&T has given seed money to community-based child care centers to set up or expand services in areas where a large number of the company's employees work. American Express has given funds to family day care associations to help them attract and train new providers. Corporate involvement tends to increase both quantity and quality of child care services.

A summary of three national surveys of employer evaluations of child care initiatives indicate that these programs help attract and retain valued employees, increase morale, and reduce absenteeism (U.S. Department of Labor, 1989). The benefits in most cases outweigh the costs.

Adult Day Care

Unlike child care, adult day care may not be an important part of the workplace response to elder care. Most older adults do not live with their children; most dependent elders prefer to remain in their own homes; and the most dependent are often in nursing homes or congregate-living facilities. However, in some cases the availability of adult day care can be extremely important.

Stride Rite Corporation pioneered a program of intergenerational day care at the workplace in 1989. The company had previously offered child care for twenty years and decided to open up an adult component of the center. Approximately 24 adults share a center with more than 40 children. The center serves employees and is also open to the local community on a sliding-scale fee basis. According to a recent unpublished survey by Generations United, there are now more than 250 intergenerational care sites throughout the United States (T. Scannell, personal communication, January 5, 1992). However, many of these are located at senior housing facilities. Phoenix Memorial Hospital has been another pioneer in the development of on-site intergenerational care. Perhaps the health care industry will take the lead in this area, since there is a tremendous work force supply problem, particularly in hospitals, and such centers could become a new community service also. However, because of the particular care needs of elders, it is unlikely that adult day care will become a major factor in workplace support programs, except, perhaps, in the health care industry through preferential arrangements with community day care facilities.

Dependent Care Spending Accounts

As noted in the section on public policies, the Economic Recovery Tax Act (ERTA, 1981) allowed companies to establish dependent care assistance plans (DCAPs), which allow employees to set aside up to $5,000 in pretax income for caregiving expenses. In some cases, employers also make tax-free contributions to the employees' accounts (Galinsky et al., 1991). The Travelers Insurance Company contributes to such accounts on a scale based on salary up to a maximum of $5,000. According to the Families and Work Institute survey (Galinsky et al., 1991) and the International Foundation of Employee Benefit Plans Survey (1990), 50% to 89% of the corporations surveyed offer dependent care accounts. This benefit is fairly recent; nearly half of the DCAPs were developed after 1987 (Galinsky et al., 1991).

However, the annual usage rate of DCAPs for all employees is only 2% (Galinsky et al., 1991), and most users are employees with child care expenses (Bureau of National Affairs, 1991c; Saltford & Heck, 1990). There are at present severe regulatory restrictions on the use of such funds: a) employees with child care costs must report the provider's social security number and forgo deducting this expense on their taxes; b) employees with elder care costs must meet the strict dependency requirements described earlier; and c) all employees must forfeit account funds not used within the year. However, any unused funds each year must be spent for community services relevant to family care. Thus, employers and employees could support needed community services for children and the elderly, or assist in starting them, through such programs. DCAPs represent a major potential future source of support for care services for elders as well as children if the regulatory provisions are adapted to the needs of employees providing care to older adults.

Long-Term Care Insurance

Long-term care insurance is a relatively new product. It is developing rapidly, and more than 130 insurance companies now offer it through individual or group policies. An increasing number of corporations offer such policies to employees as part of their benefit options. A few plans include employee's close relatives as well as the employee. It is important to note that such offerings provide the employee a group rate, but the employee is almost always responsible for the entire premium. These policies provide in varied ways for nursing home care, home care, and, in some cases, for congregate care and other service options.

The advantage of long-term care insurance is that it can protect a family against costs which can exhaust the resources of a family or their elderly relative. This, of course, can prevent some very severe stresses, though that benefit to the employee and employer may take years to realize. Only in recent years has the insurance industry begun to develop long-term care options, and the quality of products is being improved constantly under the pressures of the market and of advocates for the elderly. The entire burden of cost rests on the employee for this benefit in almost all cases. One may expect that cafeteria benefit plans will increasingly include this option for employees.

TRENDS

Cafeteria Benefit Plans

Cafeteria benefit plans, or *flexible benefit plans*, give employees a choice among fringe benefits by providing a range of options that best fit their perceived needs. In most cases some core benefits are provided to all—health, minimum vacations, sick leave and pensions. Beyond these, employees receive credits based on salary and tenure with which to purchase additional options. Employers find that this approach allows them to control total costs while providing employees enhanced choice. However, with the efforts to cut health benefit costs and increase employee contributions, exclusions, etc., many employees may find that while they are gaining more choice they may also wind up with either a significantly reduced health benefit or one that costs more out of pocket. Di Bernardino (1988) found that 22% of companies with more than 1,000 employees offer such plans and he projected that 33% of them would have cafeteria plans by 1990. The smaller company may not have the human resource staff capacity to effectively educate employees about a range of options. Likewise, companies with a high proportion of unskilled labor or employees with low literacy skills may be better served with a very simple fixed benefit approach (A. Mowbray, personal communication, May 16, 1992).

Family-Related Insurance Benefits

We can expect that options which are fully paid by the employee, such as long-term care insurance, will become increasingly popular with human resource managers. It seems safe to predict that the majority of large companies will offer this option within the next few years. The Clinton administration is also showing some interest in this area as part of their universal health insurance plan. Increasing competition among providers should help ensure that the quality of long-term care coverage offered will improve significantly. As experience with payouts occurs over the next decade, companies will also be more competitive in the pricing of such insurance.

If long-term care insurance proves both popular and financially viable, insurers will seek to create other risk pools for family related needs of employees. Thus, the insurance industry may become a major engine of growth in risk coverage for employee caregivers—for example, coverage may be developed which would provide salary replacement for a caregiver who has to take time off for family emergencies. (Current leave policies tend to provide leave time without compensation.)

In the area of elder care, we can expect that the multi-year care obligations of most caregivers (5.5 to 6.5 years on average according to Wagner et al., [1989]) will be recognized. Such long commitments mean that service options (home care, transportation, adult day care) may be more relevant to the caregiver after the early period of search for information than the information and referral services which are the current mainstay of corporate response. Companies may be able to make use of synergies between their health benefit preferred provider strategy and their family support programs. Why not establish preferred providers in adult day care and home care as a group plan option fully paid by the employee? Indeed, just as federal and state policies will favor community care, so, too, health insurance coverage can also be expected to offer incentives for less expensive home care.

Adult dependents between 18 and 65 years of age are presently little recognized in work–family policies, although the shift to "dependent care policies" certainly means that their caregivers can get access to leave policies which formerly were only available for child care. Because permanently disabled adults are the fastest growing group of dependents—and research is already clarifying that a proportion of employees carry caregiving responsibilities toward them—we can expect that the specific needs of these caregivers will be recognized and programs (educational activities, support groups, etc.) will be established to meet their needs.

Finally, with the advent of the sandwich generation, many workers carry care responsibilities towards more than one generation. We will become increasingly sophisticated in the targeting of services to the heavily burdened employee. We know, for example, that those who provide care to elders in their own homes spend significantly more hours in the provision of care and also spend significantly more dollars from their own resources than do other elder care providers (Fairfax Area Agency on Aging, 1991). Rather than offering a broad-brush approach only, employers may seek to offer targeted help to high-risk caregivers, and thus reduce the workplace impact of caregiving roles.

While vendors of services to the workplace proliferate, there may emerge a growing trend toward public–private partnership in responding to the family care obligations of workers. A number of public agencies are presently providing leadership in this area, although almost all of them are local in nature. State and federal initiatives, however, which involve collaboration with company human resource programs, may get underway in the near future (see Chapter 8).

Community Involvement

A number of major corporations have involved themselves significantly in the development of community resources for employee caregivers. Chapter 8 discusses in detail the public–private partnerships and other corporate initiatives in this area.

Supervisor Training

Rodgers & Rodgers (1989) and many other experts acknowledge that the key factor in the creation of a family-friendly workplace is a sympathetic supervisor. They call for the training of supervisors as a basic component in the establishment of workplace programs. Supervisor and management training need not be a major expense. Videos are available (for example, the Puget Sound Power and Light Company has an excellent video on the problems of self-maintenance of community-based elders), and brief, written materials can be provided to outline company policy in relation to caregivers. Particular attention needs to be given to leave policies, since supervisors are likely to be the decision makers regarding employee absence. Knowledge of policy is not sufficient; the supervisor may effectively chill the use of policies by making it clear that he or she regards their use as a negative mark against the employee. Employers must, therefore, make plain through policy statements from the CEO level that a sympathetic approach is expected of supervisors.

Supervisors often are caught between lofty corporate statements of mission and policy and practical pressures to produce on schedule. It is important to provide ongoing support for family-friendly decision making through annual recognition of supervisors who make outstanding efforts in this area. The inclusion of criteria related to work–family issues in evaluations, and discussion of supervisory dilemmas at supervisor meetings on a regular basis can do much to improve supervisor performance in this arena.

Care of Disabled Adults

The fastest growing group of dependents in American families is the dependent adult group of permanently disabled persons between 18 and 65 (Feller, 1983; U.S. Bureau of the Census, 1991). Although little research has focused to date on the caregiving concerns of workers with such dependents, some preliminary data is available. As stated in Chapter 1, Neal, Chapman, Ingersoll-Dayton, Emlen, and Boise (1990) in Portland, Oregon, and the U.S. Office of Personnel Management in Washington, DC (1992), found that 3% of employee respondents have dependent-adult care responsibilities. Although these surveys are not predictive of the national incidence of such dependence, they do suggest that it is a growing concern. The caregiving employee in this situation is by definition a long-term caregiver, and has, therefore, an ongoing need for work–family policies supportive of that care. As noted in the discussion above, cafeteria plans allow for benefits tailored to the needs of smaller numbers of employees. It seems feasible to construct a response program relevant to such caregivers—even if the response is simply to include information in handbooks, or to run seminars on work–family concerns which focus on their needs.

Labor Union Involvement

Labor unions entered the work–family arena some years ago. However, in 1990, a landmark contract was negotiated between the Communications Workers of America and AT&T which specifically included elder care benefits for the first time in a labor negotiation. (See Chapter 7 on the role of unions.) That precedent is likely to be replicated throughout the communications industry and in other industries. In 1991 the Coalition of Labor Union Women published *Bargaining for Family Benefits: A Union Members Guide,* which devoted a chapter to bargaining for elder care, as well as several chapters on child care issues. Unions have also developed a variety of internal support programs for their members. The active involvement of the labor movement in negotiating elder care and child care benefits should contribute significantly to the development of such benefits even in nonunion companies because of the effects of competition.

REFERENCES

Buck Consultants. (1991). *Benefits in the 80's vs. benefits in the 90's.* New York: Author.

Bureau of National Affairs. (1988). *Employee assistance programs: Focusing on the family* (Report No. 6). Washington, DC: Author.

Bureau of National Affairs. (1991a). *BNA's directory of work and family programs.* Washington, DC: Author.

Bureau of National Affairs. (1991b). *Small business leave policies: Excerpts from a small business administration report* (Report No. 40). Washington, DC: Author.

Bureau of National Affairs. (1991c). *Eldercare: A maturing benefit* (Report No. 48). Washington, DC: Author.

Catalyst Career and Family Center. (1981). *Corporations and two-career families: Directions for the future.* New York: Author.

Child Care and Development Block Grant. (1990). Omnibus Budget Reconciliation Act of 1990. Pub L. 97-35, Title IV, Subtitle A (as amended). Pub. L. 101-508, Title V. Income Security, Human Resources and Related Programs. Nov 5, 1990. Pub. L. 102-27, Title III, April 10, 1991, 105 Stat. 153. Pub. L. 102-401. Oct 7, 1992, 106 Stat. 1959. Washington, DC: U.S. Government Printing Office.

Coalition of Labor Union Women. (1991). *Bargaining for family benefits: A union member's guide.* New York: Author.

Creedon, M. A. (1987). *Issues for an aging America: Employees and eldercare.* CT: The University of Bridgeport.

Creedon, M. A., & Tiven, M. (1989). *Eldercare in the workplace.* Washington, DC: The National Council on the Aging.

Creedon, M. A., & Tiven, M. (1991). Employees and eldercare: A growing workplace concern. *HR Horizons, 106,* 31–36.

Di Bernardino, F. J. (1988). *A survey of flexible benefit programs 1988.* New York: Foster Higgins.

Economic Recovery Tax Act of 1981. Pub. L. 97-448. Pub. L. 98-369. Title I, Title 26, Title 46. (as amended). Pub. L. 99-272. Title XIII. (as amended) Pub. L. 100-647. Title IV; Title VI (as amended), Washington, DC: U.S. Government Printing Office.

Employee Benefits Research Institute. (1988). *Dependent care: Meeting the needs of a dynamic work force* (Issue Brief No. 85), Washington, DC: Author.

Employee Benefits Research Institute. (1991). *EBRI databook on employee benefits,* Washington, DC: Author.

Fairfax Area Agency on Aging. (1991). *The missing worker: Caring for mom and dad.* Fairfax County, VA: Author.

Family and Medical Leave Act of 1993. Pub. L. 103-3, Feb. 5, 1993. 107 Stat. (Title 2; Title 5, Title 29 as amended). Washington, DC: U.S. Government Printing Co.

Federal Employees Leave Sharing Act of 1988. Pub. L. 100-566. Oct. 31, 1988. 102 Stat 2834. Title V (as amended), Washington, DC: U.S. Government Printing Co.

Feller, B. A. (1983). Americans needing help to function at home. *Advance data, 92,* 1–3.

Fernandez, J. P. (1990). *The politics and reality of family care in corporate America.* Lexington, MA: Lexington Books.

Friedman, D. E. (1991). *Linking work-family issues to the bottom line: A summary of research.* New York: The Conference Board.

Galinsky, E., Friedman, D. E., & Hernandez, C. A. (1991). *The corporate reference guide to work-family programs.* New York: Families and Work Institute.

Gorey, K. M., Brice, G. C., & Rice, R. W. (1990). An Elder care training needs assessment among employee assistance program staff. *Employee Assistance Quarterly, 5*(3), 71–93

Hansen, J. (1989, August). Editorial, *Aging Network News,* p. 1.

Hewitt Associates. (1990). *Work and family benefits provided by major U.S. employers in 1990.* Lincolnshire, IL: Author.

Hewitt Associates. (1991). *Micro-history of compensation and benefits.* Scottsdale, AZ: Author.

Human Services Reauthorization Act of 1986. Pub. L. 99-425. Sept. 30, 1986. 100 Stat. 966. (Title 7, Title 20, Title 42, as amended). Pub. L. 101-204. Title VII. Dec 7, 1989. 103 Stat. 1821 (Title

42, as amended). Pub. L. 101-501. Title VI. (as amended). Nov. 3, 1990. 104 Stat. 1257, 1258 (Title 42 as amended). Washington, DC: U.S. Government Printing Office.

International Foundation of Employee Benefit Plans. (1990). *Nontraditional benefits for the workforce of 2000.* Brookfield, WI: Author.

IRS (1981). United States Code annotated. Internal Revenue Service. Title 26, Section 129. Dependent Care Assistance Plans. Washington, DC: U.S. Government Printing Office.

Kahn, A. J., & Kamerman, S. B. (1987). *Child care choices: Facing the hard choices.* Dover, MA: Auburn House.

Keitel, R. W. (1980, September). *Quality of working life in the private sector: An overview and a developmental perspective.* Washington DC: Workforce Effectiveness and Development Group, U.S. Office of Personnel Management.

Kolodrubetz, W. W. (1972, April). Two decades of employee-benefit plans, 1950–70: A review. *Social Security Bulletin,* 10–22.

Levine, J. (1986). Fathers and the corporation. *Across the Board,* New York: Conference Board.

Magid, R. Y. (1983). *Child care initiatives for working parents: Why employers get involved. An AMA survey report.* New York: American Management Association.

Magid, R. Y. (1991). Becoming a family-responsive company: A process not a program. *HR Horizons, 106,* 7–14.

Neal, M. B. (1992). *Research findings on eldercare.* Presentation at American Society on Aging Annual Conference. San Diego.

Neal, M. B., Chapman, N., Ingersoll-Dayton, B., Emlen, A., & Boise, L. (1990). Absenteeism and stress among employed caregivers of the elderly, disabled adults, and children. In D. E. Biegel & A. Blum (Eds.), *Aging and caregiving: Theory, research, and policy* (pp. 160–183). CA: Sage.

Pregnancy Discrimination Act. Pub. L. 95-555, Oct. 31, 1978, 92 Stat. 2076. Title 42 (as amended).

Rodgers, F. S., & Rodgers, C. (1989). Business and the facts of family life. *Harvard Business Review, 67*(6), 121–129.

Saltford, N. C. & Heck, R. K. Z. (1990). *An overview of employee benefits supportive of families* (An EBRI Special Report). Washington, DC: Employee Benefits Research Institute.

Scannell, Teresa. (Jan 5, 1992). Executive Director, Generations United. Personal Communication. Washington DC.

Scharlach, A. E., Lowe, B. F., & Schneider, E. (1991). *Elder care and the workforce: Blue print for action.* Lexington, MA: Lexington Books.

Seidman, Jane. Director, Work and Family Programs, Office of Personnel Management. (1994, Jan. 28). Washington, D.C. Personal Communication.

Travelers Insurance Company (1985). The Travelers employee caregiver study. Hartford, CT: Author.

U.S. Bureau of the Census. (1991). *Population profile of the United States: 1991* (Current Population Reports, Series p. 23, no. 173). Washington, DC: U.S. Government Printing Office.

U.S. Bureau of the Census. (1992). *Household, families, and children: A 30 year perspective* (Current Population Reports, Series P-23, No. 181). Washington, DC: U.S. Government Printing Office.

U.S. Chamber of Commerce. (1986). *Employee Benefits*, Washington, DC: Author.

U.S. Department of Labor, Women's Bureau. (1989). *Employers and child care: Benefiting work and family.* Washington, DC: U.S. Government Printing Office.

U.S. Merit Systems Protection Board. (1991, November). *Balancing work responsibilities and family needs: the federal civil service response. A report to the President and Congress of the United States.* Washington, DC: U.S. Government Printing Office.

U.S. Office of Personnel Management. (1992 April). The study of the work and family needs of the federal work force: A report to Congress. Washington, DC: Office of Work and Family, U.S. Office of Personnel Management.

Wagner, D. L., Creedon, M. A., Sasala, J. M., & Neal, M. B. (1989). *Employees and eldercare: Designing effective responses for the workplace.* CT: The University of Bridgeport.

Wiatrowski, W. J. (1990). Family-Related Benefits in the Workplace. *Monthly Labor Review, 113*(3), 28–33.

Zigler, E. F., & Lang, M. E. (1991). *Child care choices: Balancing the needs of children, families, and society.* New York: The Free Press.

5 EAPs and Work and Family Programs

This chapter examines the integration of work and family programs into the EAP. After presenting some background information, it describes two EAPs that have developed work and family programs—one union and one corporate. Next, it examines historical and contemporary factors that affect EAP responses to work and family issues. It then offers suggestions on ways to improve EAP responses to work and family concerns. The chapter ends with a discussion of the promise of EAPs in the work and family area.

BACKGROUND INFORMATION

An Employee Assistance Program (EAP) consists of a collection of services provided by employers or unions to employees with personal concerns or problems that may affect job performance. Union EAPs are generally referred to as member assistance programs (MAPs). To ease readability, though, the term EAP is used to refer to union and corporate programs.

Typical EAP services include assessment and referral, personal and family counseling, educational seminars, supervisory training, and organizational development. The confidential counseling and referral services are often extended to family members. Most EAPs offer from one to three counseling sessions and refer employees to outside agencies if longer intervention is needed.

The EAP is a natural place for offering assistance to employed caregivers. Well trained EAP professionals can help employed caregivers locate appropriate community resources for themselves, their children, disabled relatives, and frail elders. They can offer lunch time seminars on topics related to work and family issues. Informed EAP professionals can explain workplace programs as well as government legislation and tax laws relevant to dependent care. If brief counseling is necessary, they can offer this too. EAPs with upper management support can make policy recommendations (e.g., flextime or supervisory sensitivity training sessions) to the employer to improve support to employed caregivers.

EAP services have been found to reduce the on-the-job time employed caregivers spend looking for resources. They also lower caregiver frustrations that can detract from work performance. In one survey of almost 2,000 employees who cared for frail relatives, 59% of the respondents found the EAP services helpful to them (Scharlach & Boyd, 1989).

Recent evaluation studies suggest that EAPs are cost effective. McDonnell Douglas's (MDD) well publicized cost benefit analysis revealed their EAP would save the company six million dollars within a four-year period. Savings were based on decreased absenteeism and lowered health care costs (Stuart, 1993).

EAPs have become very popular. The Bureau of National Affairs (1987) reported that 80% of the *Fortune* 500 companies sponsored EAPs in 1987. Hays Huggins Company surveyed over 1,000 organizations and found that 65% of them offered EAPs in 1992 compared to only 43% in 1987 (National Underwriter, 1992).

Many EAPs have expanded their role to include programs that deal specifically with employed caregivers (Wojcik, 1992). The Families and Work Institute's survey of the largest *Fortune* 1,000 companies in 30 industry areas reported that 86% of them offered EAP services as part of their work and family program (Galinsky, Friedman, & Hernandez, 1991). Because specific services were not defined, the type and extent of assistance to employed caregivers was unclear.

EAP MODELS

EAP services can be provided by staff from within the organization, staff from an external EAP, or staff provided through a consortium arrangement. A consortium is set up when small businesses pool their resources to purchase EAP services from an outside vendor. Some work organizations have both an internal EAP as well as an external vendor. Organizational size, location, and structure often determine the particular model. A national survey of corporate EAPs found that 44.5% of EAPs were internal and 55.5% were external (Employee Benefits BASICS, 1991).

Internal EAPs usually have only two or three staff members. They are located in human resources/personnel or medical departments. External EAPs vary in size—those with a national scope are large, while local vendors are smaller. Union based EAPs or MAPs are frequently located in the welfare/benefits fund office.

Although there are many EAPs that offer assistance to employees with work and family concerns, two are highlighted here. They are selected because they represent typical characteristics of union and corporate settings.

Union Model: The Work and Family Assistance Program

The Work and Family Assistance Program (WFAP) is a labor consortium made up of the United Staff Association AFT Local 3882 Member Assistance Program and the Oil, Chemical and Atomic Workers Local 8–149 Work and Family Program. WFAP provides information, intervention, referral and follow up for the union members of ten employers. It is a volunteer-based program coordinated by a professional social worker (Work and Family Assistance Program, unpublished).

Volunteers are union members who have received 20 hours of training in communication skills, locating resources, confidentiality, handling stress, and several other topics. Volunteers primarily offer support and make referrals to community resources. If further assessment and intervention is needed, the members are referred to the social worker who has a masters in social work. Using trained volunteers is very cost effective and it also promotes good will among union members.

The WFAP also offers presentations and workshops on work and family concerns and other topics such as substance abuse and credit and budget information. In 1992, 6% of the membership utilized the WFAP.

The WFAP was successful in getting the employers to recognize the legitimacy of work and family issues. Prior to their involvement, some employers had rigid time expectations of their workers and they would discipline them for taking time off for family responsibilities. As a result of the efforts of WFAP, workers have a more flexible schedule and are not disciplined for lateness due to family duties. The worker and employer try to resolve together the work and family time conflicts (L. May, personal communication, March, 1993). Thus, even with a skeleton staff, the unions in the labor consortium offer a range of important services.

Corporate Model: Hoffman-La Roche's Eldercare Program

The EAP at Hoffman-La Roche was established in 1979, initially as a contracted outside service. Eventually, it evolved into an internal program. The EAP serves 6,000 local and 11,000 nationwide employees. Eighty percent of the employees seen at the EAP are self-referrals, with the remainder referred to the EAP by medical department staff, human resource staff, or the supervisor.

The staff consist of four professionals, two fulltime, including the administrator, and two parttime consultants. They all have master degrees or higher in psychology or social work (McCrae, 1991).

Since inception, the EAP at Hoffman-La Roche has offered education, counseling, and referral services to employees who care for children, persons with disabilities, and frail relatives. They formalized their elder care services in 1990 after learning that the average age of their employees was 43 years old, a typical age when caregiving duties begin.

Eldercare Program. The Eldercare Program at Hoffman-La Roche has several components: assessment and evaluation of elder care needs and resources, provision of direct services to employees and their family members; and organizational development (Strazdas, 1992). The assessment component included a survey of attendees at elder care events in 1991 to determine their need for assistance. This information was then used to develop a carefully screened and continuously monitored list of elder care providers.

Direct services to employees and their family members include hosting caregiver resource information fairs and convening evening and lunch time seminars on topics related to aging and caring for the aged (e.g., long-term care insurance, nursing home placement, living wills). Short-term counseling and referral are also an integral part of the service package. The EAP contracted with Senior Services (a resource and referral elder care service) to provide specialized counseling to employees and to conduct their evening series on caring for the aged.

The organizational development component involved several steps. One of the most important was setting up a small committee of staff from the EAP, Benefits, and Employee Relations departments to plan and coordinate the eldercare program. Improved interdepartmental communication, efficiency, and goodwill were gained by that process. The committee investigated what similar workplaces (competitors) were providing to their employees. Efforts were also put into marketing the Eldercare Program aggressively and attractively. This has paid off—referrals to the EAP concerning elder care concerns went from 4% in 1990 to 10.6% in 1992 (Strazdas, 1992). By several indications, employees who have participated in the elder care services have judged their experience helpful to them in managing work while caring for an aging relative.

FORCES SHAPING EAP RESPONSES

As seen in the union and corporate models just presented, EAPs vary considerably from one another in both their organizational role and in services provided. EAPs have been and continue to be shaped by many forces: ideology, organizational climate, union versus corporate affiliation, government legislation, and technology. This next section reviews these major forces and their impact on the integration of work and family concerns into the EAP.

Ideology

Values and beliefs (ideology) about the primary purpose of EAPs influence the types of employees they reach out to and the services they provide (Googins & Godfrey, 1987). Work and family programs fit best in EAPs with a "broad-brush" ideology that allow them to reach out to all employees, sick and well, and to focus on workplace and community development in addition to individual problem solving. Most EAPs today target all employees and some attempt to modify work and community environments to be more responsive to the needs of employed caregivers.

Two approaches, however, alcohol treatment and managed care, present in some EAPs, may present difficulties in the integration of work and family programs. They are discussed in the next section.

Serving the troubled employee. The early EAPs, known as occupational alcoholism programs (OAP), were developed in the 1940s to serve employees with drinking problems. Because alcoholics use a lot of denial, supervisors were the primary referral source (Henderson & Bacon, 1953). Supervisors were trained to recognize certain job performance problems: absenteeism, lateness, and sick leave and to use them as the basis for referrals to the OAP.

EAPs that primarily reach out to troubled employees and emphasize supervisory referrals based on work absences may discourage employed caregivers from seeking out their EAP. Most employed caregivers do not see themselves as "troubled employees," but as healthy employees struggling with stressful life events. Prevention services such as lunch time seminars on managing work and caregiving and help with locating child care and elder care services are the most useful to them. For employed caregivers, supervisory referrals are generally not necessary. In most cases, employed caregivers will feel comfortable referring themselves to the EAP, particularly when their workplaces have made a commitment to work and family issues.

Absenteeism among employed caregivers can be seen as not only a personal problem but possibly a workplace structural problem. The solutions are often found in policy changes that offer a more flexible work schedule. Additionally, several researchers have reported that among women with young children absenteeism is a stress buffer, enabling them to more successfully manage their joint tasks (Neal, Chapman, Ingersoll-Dayton, & Emlen, 1993).

Managed care. Presently, managed care is in vogue, influenced by employers' drastically rising health insurance costs. Managed care programs are set up to monitor and sometimes control and limit the utilization of health and mental health services. Health maintenance organizations (HMOs) and insurance companies with mandatory preadmission review procedures are examples of managed care programs.

Interestingly, EAPs can be seen as the original managed care programs. Many EAPs set up preferred provider lists, use them for referrals, and then inquire about employee satisfaction with referred service. In this way they act as gatekeepers of health care services. Although EAPs perform these functions, they generally do not deny services, an important component of today's managed care programs. EAP staff, accustomed to locating services, not denying them, may feel conflict in this new role. The two roles do not have to be incompatible, however. Carefully screened and monitored providers are more likely to provide better care (Scanlon, 1992).

Organizational Climate

EAPs vary not only in program ideology and design, but in their status and position within the work organization's hierarchy. For example, EAPs with low status will have a very difficult time convincing upper management to pay for staff training to increase staff's competency in helping employees with work and family concerns. They may also be excluded from upper management's dealings with outside vendors selected to provide resource and referral services for employees caring for children and frail elders.

On the other hand, EAPs held in high esteem will be actively involved in all phases of the company or union's expansion of work and family programs. EAP staff can play a vital role in developing employee needs assessments, recommending organizational changes, and collaborating on work and family issues with other internal departments such as medical, compensation and benefits, and human resources, or with outside vendors.

Corporate or union climate is another factor that influences the expansion of work and family programs within EAPs. Work organizations that view family issues as legitimate business concerns are the most receptive to change. In mildly resistant organizations, EAP managers will need to convince CEOs, upper management, and union officials of the advantages of work and family programs. EAPs in unreceptive work environments may be limited in what they can accomplish until attitude changes occur either through outside government intervention or some external event that permits a fresh look at existing problems.

Union-based versus Corporate-based EAPs

Unions were slow to get involved in the EAP movement because they saw EAPs as threats to individual rights (Bickerton, 1991). They feared that companies would use EAPs as a mechanism to justify firing an employee and for other disciplinary measures. They also feared that by participating with management in forming joint EAPs, they could be coopted by them and lose sight of their advocacy activities (Steele, 1989).

Many of the goals of EAPs, however, are consistent with union goals: job security and job performance, workplace cohesiveness, and early intervention with work or personal problems to avoid termination or later health problems (Bickerton, 1991). Thus, it was just a matter of time before unions set up their own EAPs or developed joint programs with management.

Because unions are established to protect workers, their focus is more on individual needs than on those of the organization. Unions have been very effective in negotiating family-focused workplace policies and benefits that have improved the conditions of employed caregivers (*Bargaining for Family*

Benefits, 1991). Union EAPs are in a better position than corporate EAPs to bring about organizational changes on behalf of employed caregivers.

Government Legislation

Two important laws have been passed that have expanded the number of EAPs as well as modified program design. The first, the Comprehensive Alcohol Abuse and Alcoholism Prevention, Treatment and Rehabilitation Act of 1970 (Hughes Act), not only changed the focus of EAPs, but contributed to the largest growth ever of new programs. This legislation mandated that all federal agencies and the military implement alcoholism programs. It also encouraged all other work organizations to do likewise. For example, all work organizations, not just federal agencies, were offered technical assistance in establishing new programs. Additionally, funds were set aside for EAP demonstration projects and research.

With this legislation, occupational alcohol programs were renamed employee assistance programs (EAP). These new programs were expected to broaden their scope beyond alcoholism to include a range of personal and work-related problems that affect job performance. Thus, EAPs began reaching out to a larger number of employees. The primary target was still the alcoholic, but a wider net was cast to reduce the stigma of getting help. It was also hoped that this approach would get employees into EAPs who, in addition to the presenting problem, had problems with drinking (Masi, 1984). Consistent with this new program design, self-referrals were encouraged. The EAP's focus, though, was still on the troubled employee.

The next important legislation was the Drug Free Workplace Act of 1988, which requires federal agencies and firms under government contract to provide their employees with access to EAP services (Stuart, 1993). Once again, EAPs grew rapidly in response to government mandates. Many work organizations implemented drug testing programs as part of their EAP service. Such policies, though, have implications for trust, confidentiality, and neutrality which can adversely affect service utilization. Employees may avoid EAPs that are seen as potential threats to their personal freedom and job security. Thus, many new programs cropped up, but some may have affected the willingness of workers with family concerns to affiliate with them, setting services back rather than ahead.

With today's concern about the cost of health care, future government legislation may push EAPs into mandated managed care programs. This change, as discussed earlier, may create potential conflicts for EAP staff.

Technology

The provision of resource and referral services for employees caring for children and frail elders has become a big business. It is very difficult for most EAPs to devote the considerable time required to organize computerized, up-to-date, quality resource information on a regional or national scale. In most cases it is cost effective for work organizations to contract out for this service. Problems occur, though, when R&R agencies have little communication with the employing EAP. Client confidentiality makes open communication difficult but not impossible. At the very least, the external R&R vendor should refer an employee with additional concerns to the EAP. Accountability policies and mechanisms need to be set up to ensure that appropriate communication takes place.

National EAPs offer assessment and referral as well as counseling on the telephone. They rarely provide the more intimate face-to-face interview. Phone interventions are cost effective in the short run, but they raise questions about long-term effectiveness in comparison with in-person services. Comparative research on this topic is lacking, even though some experts in human resources believe that in ten years EAPs will be limited to a handful of national EAPs that provide the bulk of their services on the phone (Kertesz, 1992).

STRENGTHENING EAP RESPONSES

Employee Needs Assessment

One of the quickest ways for an EAP to determine needs of employed caregivers is to examine their own intake and utilization data. Patterns of resource and counseling requests can be identified. Personnel, human resources, and medical departments are additional sources of data. Specific questions on caregiving situations can be added to intake forms, if they do not already exist. Robert Wilson's experiences at Travelers taught him that it was crucial to include this tracking information (personal communication, June 15, 1991).

Conducting an employee needs assessment is one of the best ways to find out more specifically how the EAP can help the majority of employees better manage their work and family responsibilities. Appendix B presents a sample needs assessment and Chapter 9 discusses ways to implement work and family programs in unions and work organizations. Besides surveys, EAPs can conduct focus groups with employees to supplement and enrich information gathered from surveys and in-house data.

In-Service Training

In the only known survey of EAP staff, Gorey, Brice, and Rice (1990), found that 60% of the sample reported low competency in dealing with employee questions and concerns about caring for frail relatives. For example, 81% could not explain how "spend down" for Medicaid worked and 57% were unable to advise on long-term care options. Gorey and colleagues estimate that two full days of in-service training could greatly improve staff's ability to help employed caregivers of frail relatives. In order for this to happen, though, work organizations must be willing to make the relatively small financial commitment for in-service training.

Expansion and Coordination of Services

When EAPs add work and family programs, it is very important to think through how these modifications affect other departments within the work organization. Otherwise, conflicts over turf issues can come up and create delays in the development of work and family programs. Potential conflicts should be dealt with early and as directly as possible. A related problem that could arise is the duplication of services which could lead to decreased efficiency, increased costs, and fragmentation of services. To avoid this, EAP administrators should be familiar with family-focused benefits and services provided by personnel, human resources, and/or the medical departments within the organization. They should also keep other departments abreast of their developments and seek input from them.

Communication is the key to successful program development. All departments should be talking to one another about any proposed changes in the scope of the EAP. Once new programs are implemented, it is especially important to inform employees of new developments and remind them periodically of current programs.

Advocacy

The WFAP, discussed earlier, operated as a change agent when they negotiated a more flexible work schedule for their union members. The EAP at Hoffman-La Roche worked closely with upper management to implement the Eldercare Program. EAP staff are in a good position to identify workplace, government, and community policies and services that hinder employed caregivers' success in balancing work and family responsibilities. In order to become an advocate for employed caregivers, however, EAP staff must view themselves as change agents as well as enablers (Akabas, 1990; Balgopal, 1989; Kurzman & Akabas, 1981. In this expanded role, they can work toward influencing workplace and government policies on behalf of employed caregivers.

All EAPs can help ensure that their work organizations prepare for and inform employees of their rights to 12 weeks of unpaid leave with job guarantee, under the Family and Medical Leave Act of 1993. Oftentimes employees are unaware of family focused policies, benefits, and services offered at their workplaces or unions. The EAP, as an advocate for working families, can help ensure efforts are made by the company to inform them of their benefits and services.

Program Evaluation

Most EAPs track utilization data (number of cases seen, presenting problem, and outcome) and some assess employees' satisfaction with services. These program evaluations, however, do not inform the EAP of success in reducing absenteeism and health care costs.

The best program evaluation studies, unfortunately, are time consuming and costly. An example of an excellent study was the one conducted by McDonnell Douglas. It measured absenteeism rates and health care costs among a large number of employees and compared EAP users with all other employees over a long period of time (Scanlon, 1992). Unions and companies interested in high-quality evaluations will need to provide the economic resources to develop staff expertise or work with outside bodies such as colleges, universities or consulting organizations.

External EAP Vendors

EAP staff can not be expected to be experts in everything. Many companies have decided to contract with outside vendors in order to meet some of their employees' needs. There are about 10,000 vendors to choose from (Rosenzweig & Kramer, 1992). The most frequently requested services are for resource and referral (R&R), especially if the work organization is national in scope. Internal EAPs should be involved in the planning and selection phases, for here again communication is critical. Referral mechanisms between the internal EAP and outside vendor need to be in place.

Future projections indicate that R&R for child care and elder care community resources will be handled by public agencies such as local area agencies on aging. Thus, when considering contracting with private vendors, the public domain may provide a cost effective resource for basic information. However, more intensive R&R may require a national and/or specialized resource that may be either profit or not-for-profit. (See Chapter 6 on vendors.)

National and State Leadership

At least three professional associations, the Employee Assistance Professionals Association (EAPA), the National Association of Social Workers (NASW), and the Employee Assistance Society of North America (EASNA) offer guidance to EAP professionals. EAPA is the most influential because it sets professional standards and credentialing requirements. It also offers research and educational activities to its members. National associations such as NASW and EAPA can serve very important functions by providing coordination, education, standard setting, and research activities for EAP professionals throughout the country. Unfortunately, many EAP personnel are not affiliated with these associations.

Key professionals within these associations have provided some leadership. In the social work area, several professors and heads of university occupational social work research centers have written extensively on the subject of EAPs. They have also helped to establish work and family committees at the local NASW chapters. Social workers with a masters degree and a specialization in policy and practice of occupational social work are well prepared to work in the EAP field. They can assess and intervene at both the clinical and policy levels (Kurzman, 1993).

On the state level, California has required external EAP vendors to obtain licenses and to demonstrate financial stability in an effort to provide quality control of the delivery of services to employees (Kertesz, 1992). With the growth of EAPs and the increasing extensiveness of their services, more organized leadership is needed.

PROMISE OF EAPS IN WORK AND FAMILY AREA

As demonstrated throughout this book, families and workplaces are interdependent. As Googins (1991, p. 8) notes, "the work system cannot exist unless it draws on the family system for its labor pool." And families need the income and fringe benefits that the workplace provides. Yet, problems arise for each system as they try to meet their goals. EAPs are well suited, as demonstrated in this chapter, to help employees and their family members and the work organizations that employ them find solutions to work and family dilemmas.

Well-trained EAP staff, especially those in broad-brush in-house units, are cognizant of the work organization's cultural climate, managerial styles, financial strength, and other resources and demands. They are familiar with employees' family concerns, work–family struggles, problems locating suitable resources, and other problems. This centrality makes EAPs essential players in helping work organizations and their employees find solutions that enhance the quality of employees' and their families' lives, while at the same time contributing to the success of the work organization.

REFERENCES

Akabas, S. H. (1990). Reconciling the demands of work with the needs of families. *Families in Society: The Journal of Contemporary Human Services, 71*, 366–371.

Balgopal, P. R. (1989). Occupational social work: An expanded clinical perspective. *Social Work, 34*, 437–442.

Bargaining for family benefits: A union member's guide. (1991). New York: Coalition of Labor Union Women.

Bickerton, R. L. (1991). Employee assistance: A History in progress. *EAP Digest, 11*(1), 34–42, 82–84, 91.

Bureau of National Affairs. 1987. *Employee Assistance Programs: Benefits, problems, and prospects*. Washington, DC: Author.

Comprehensive Alcohol Abuse and Alcoholism Prevention, Treatment and Rehabilitation of 1970 (Hughes Act), 42 U.S.C. §4582.

Employee Benefits BASICS (1991). *Employee Assistance Programs.* Brookfield, WI: International Foundation of Employee Benefit Plans.

Family and Medical Leave Act of 1993. Pub. L. 103-3, Feb. 5, 1993. 107 Stat. (Title 2; Title 5, Title 29 as amended). Washington, DC: U.S. Government Printing Co.

Galinsky, E., Friedman, D. E., & Hernandez, C. A. (1991). *The corporate reference guide to work-family programs*. New York: Families and Work Institute.

Googins, B. K. (1991). *Work/family conflicts: Private live, public responses*. Westport, CT: Auburn House.

Googins, B. K., & Godfrey, J. (1987). *Occupational social work*. Englewood Cliffs, NJ: Prentice Hall.

Gorey, K. M., Brice, G. C., & Rice, R.W. (1990). An elder care training needs assessment among employee assistance program staff. *Employee Assistance Quarterly, 5*(3), 71–93.

Henderson, R. M., & Bacon, S. D. (1953). Problem drinking: The Yale Plan for Business and Industry. *Quarterly Journal of Studies on Alcohol, 14*, 247–262.

Kurzman, P. A. (1993). Employee assistance programs: Toward a comprehensive service model. In P. A. Kurzman & S. H. Akabas (Eds.), *Work and well-being: The occupational social work advantage* (pp. 26–45). Washington, DC: National Association of Social Workers Press.

Kertesz, L. (1992). Discovering the many and varied uses of EAPs. *Business Insurance, 26*(23), 57.

Kurzman, P. A., & Akabas, S. H. (1981). Industrial social work as an arena for practice. *Social Work, 26*, 52–60.

McCrae, S. (1991). The EAP: Helping to lighten the load. *Inside Roche, 15*, 2–11.

Masi, D. A. (1984). *Designing employee assistance programs.* New York: American Management Association.

National Underwriter. (1992, February 24). 65 percent of cos. provide EAPs: Survey. 96, 9.

Neal, M. B., Chapman, N. J., Ingersoll-Dayton, B., & Emlen, A. C. (1993). *Balancing work and caregiving for children, adults, and elders.* Newbury Park, CA: Sage.

Rosenzweig, S. & Kramer, E. P. (1992). Human Resources: Get with the program. *Small Business Reports, 17*(8), 20–24.

Scanlon, W. F. (1992). EAPs emerge triumphant in an era of cost containment. *Managing Employee Health Benefits, 1*(1), 69–75.

Scharlach, A. E., & Boyd, S. (1989). Caregiving and employment: Results of an employee survey. *The Gerontologist, 29*, 382–387.

Steele, P. D. (1989). A history of job-based alcoholism programs: 1955–1972. *The Journal of Drug Issues, 19*, 511–532.

Strazdas, S. (1992, October). *A corporate, internal employee assistance program approach to eldercare.* Presentation at the New Jersey Task Force on Employer Supported Family Initiatives on Work and Family Strategies, Somerset, New Jersey.

Stuart, P. (1993). Investments in EAPs pay off. *Personnel Journal, 72*(2), 43–49, 51–52, 54.

Wojcik, J. (1992). Expanded EAP role benefits employers and employees. *Business Insurance, 26*(23), 3, 21–23.

Work and Family Assistance Program. (unpublished brochure). Member Assistance Program, The United Staff Association of New York University, AFT Local 3882. New York, NY.

6 The Vendor Community

Much has been written about the needs of working caregivers of children and/or elders, but there has been little focus in the literature on the vendor community. This is unfortunate, because vendors have a major influence on what employers offer to their employees; they also act as advocates (perhaps the most effective advocates) for services and workplace policies which may become the centerpieces of work and family programs in the future. Vendors are more sensitive to market realities than academics and are often much more skilled at "selling" employers on the need for services than professionals in traditional community services. Their ultimate discipline is economic survival. Vendors are any public, profit, and not-for-profit organization that provides services to corporations.

There are presently more than 10,000 vendors of employee assistance services (Rosenzweig & Kramer, 1992), so human resource executives seeking outside assistance in the provision of family supports to employees would do well to heed the warning contained in the 1989 *Directory of Providers Offering Eldercare Services* published by the Health Action Forum of Greater Boston: "It is important that you thoroughly investigate providers you are considering and ask for references" (p. 1). The authors point out that some providers listed in the *Directory* had been providing services to elders and their families for years while others were brand new organizations without any corporate or other clients.

This chapter will discuss a variety of services and will cite some vendors as examples. However, there is no intention to endorse any vendor over other providers, although those which have been cited are well known in the field.

RESEARCH AND PROGRAM DESIGN

Many companies are only now considering what support programs they might offer in the work and family area. A survey of employees regarding their needs and wishes may be an important starting point, and certainly close attention must be paid to corporate demographics (age, male to female ratio, etc.), corporate traditions, and both internal resources and community resources. Such research and planning tasks may be carried out with the help of organizations like the Families and Work Institute in New York, the Boston University Center on Work and Family, Portland State University's Regional Research Institute for Human Services, or consulting bodies such as Burud and Associates in Los Angeles, Initiatives in Doylestown, Pennsylvania, or the Creedon Group in Vienna, Virginia. Fees for research and planning services can vary greatly. The authors have heard of fees as large as $2.5 million for one company with more than 60,000 employees. However, it should be possible to find such services for much more modest fees.

EMPLOYEE ASSISTANCE PROGRAMS

Vendors have been active in the provision of employee assistance programs since the inception of this benefit. Experts estimate that 50% of all EAP services are provided by outside vendors, some of them local providers and others nationwide in scope.

EAP providers are developing internal capacity regarding child care and elder care information and referral and some are establishing relationships with vendors of such expertise. Just recently a growing trend has emerged for corporations to market their internal expertise in these areas to other companies. Examples include the Center for Corporate Health established by Travelers Insurance, and the 1992 announcement by IBM of the establishment of a human resources subsidiary called "Workforce Solutions" (*New York Times*, May 8, 1992). When a computer industry giant such as IBM, or an insurance industry leader like Travelers, begins vending human resource expertise, they do so because they think that a market exists for these services.

It is important to realize that personnel costs are approximately 70% of total costs for most businesses, and within personnel costs, benefits make up some 30% of the total. Within the broad field of benefits, health care insurance consumes more than half of the total. Indeed health benefit costs are rising at an uncontrolled pace, and many companies are shifting more and more of the cost of this benefit onto the shoulders of workers. As noted in Chapter 4, many benefits executives regard work–family support programs as relatively inexpensive and controllable costs. For some executives it may be strategic to offer such programs at the same time as limits are placed on health benefits. It is difficult to estimate the total cost of work–family benefits in the United States, but it is certainly more than 100 million dollars per year and growing rapidly. This indicates that there is a substantial market for EAP services provided by vendors.

WORK–FAMILY COORDINATORS

A recent study by the Conference Board (1991) estimates that some 300 companies have hired work–family coordinators. The majority of these program directors have been drawn from internal human resource staff; indeed the majority of these professionals have MBA degrees. Other companies, such as Polaroid and Marriott, have hired individuals with child care or elder care expertise and professional credentials in social work, counseling, and related fields. The rapid growth in such hiring suggests that work and family programs are becoming permanent components of the human resource function. Estimates provided by the Conference Board suggest that the average salary for this position is $56,000. This position and support staff, therefore, require a program budget in excess of $100,000. It presents a highly visible symbol of corporate commitment to family support programs. Some companies (Polaroid, for example) have added child, family, and elder care expertise to the Employee Assistance Program staff on either a fulltime or parttime basis (L. Slovic, personal communication, May 5, 1992).

RESOURCE AND REFERRAL

The most popular service adopted by U.S. corporations, known as *resource and referral* (R&R) or information and referral (I&R), was initiated for child care in 1983 and for elder care around 1986. Because companies with multiple locations may require data bases on services for dependents of employees on a nationwide basis, and older relatives may often live at a distance from adult children, it was, perhaps, inevitable that this service would be sought from external resources. IBM is recognized as a pioneer in this area for child care and later (1988) for elder care, with Work Family Directions of Brookline, Massachusetts, as the vendor. However, the first I&R program for elder care, to our knowledge, was offered by Hallmark in Kansas City, with Family and Children's Service of Kansas City as the vendor.

In the R&R business there are now hundreds of vendors. NACRA, The National Association of Child Care Resource and Referral Agencies, currently has a membership of more than 500 service providers. These range in size from very small local agencies to national organizations with hundreds of local subcontractors. The membership also includes profit, not-for-profit, and public agencies. This chapter will provide a brief description of some of the providers in each category.

Among the best known vendors in this field are Work Family Directions, which offers service to IBM, Travelers, AT&T, and a large number of smaller companies. The Partnership Group in Lansdale, Pennsylvania, is another national vendor of both child and elder care resource and referral. The Dependent Care Connection, Westport, Connecticut, also offers national service for both children and elders. Not-for-profit national vendors include Family Service America (both child and elder) and the National Association of Area Agencies on Aging (elder).

Prices for R&R or I&R are closely held information. However, estimates usually run from $10 to $15 per employee on an annual capitation fee basis for either child or elder R&R service. It is also important to note that "enhanced" R&R, which requires more time spent in telephone counseling, is more expensive. A simple R&R service, offering information about resources only, will be less expensive. Some vendors are willing to provide these services on a more flexible basis (e.g., a flat annual fee plus a small fee per individual served). Because some regions of the country, such as the Northeast, are more expensive than others, such as the Midwest or South, companies that are concentrated in lower cost regions may be able to negotiate a somewhat lower cost structure.

CONSULTATION RESOURCES

There is also a very wide range of organizations and individuals providing consultation on child care and/or elder care. (See Appendix A.) The Association of Child Care Consultants Inc. (ACCI), for example, presently has several hundred members. Such organizations as Mercer, Meidinger, Hansen; Wyatt; Hewitt Associates, and other major corporate consulting firms now offer work–family consultation. Organizations such as the Families and Work Institute have been established specifically to carry out research and consultation on work–family issues.

Universities and colleges have also become a resource for employee surveys, educational programs for employees, program evaluation, and other services. Among the premier providers of such services are the Boston University Center on Work and Family, the Bank Street College of Education in New York City, and the Portland State University Regional Training Center in Portland, Oregon. There are many other colleges and universities with individual faculty members or particular departments bearing outstanding credentials on work and family issues. A company or trade union might begin by checking for such resources in the local community.

CHILD CARE SERVICES

Day Care Service

This service is presently offered primarily for children, although a number of organizations offer intergenerational care (Stride Rite and Phoenix Memorial Hospital are two examples). Consortia of companies in Tysons Corner, Virginia, and other locations sponsor child care centers. Some organizations are large enough to sponsor internal child care centers. In 1992, the Port Authority of New York opened a child care center at Kennedy Airport in New York for employees of the various companies using Kennedy. The Social Security Administration similarly established a child care center at its headquarters in Baltimore.

Business or office parks are more frequently designing day care centers for children into the park amenities (Fernandez, 1990). Many companies have established relationships with local not-for-profit day care centers and assist employees to obtain pre-tax service for their children through the Dependent Care Assistance Plan mechanism. Others develop preferred provider contracts with child care chains, and provide vouchers to employees which allow them to obtain day care for their children at lower cost (Smith, 1991). Companies with flexible spending accounts provide employees the opportunity to target up to $5,000 from salary tax free for child care or other dependent care services. This allows employees to choose their own day care vendor. Presently the vast majority of these accounts are utilized for child care services only.

Many day care providers are sponsored by local not-for-profit organizations such as churches or synagogues, others such as Kinder Care are national chains. The price of day care service varies greatly, depending on region of the country, sponsorship, personnel, and other factors.

One of the major problems for working parents, as discussed in Chapter 2, is the availability of quality child care service. A national consortium of companies, the American Business Collaboration for Quality Dependent Care, with Work Family Directions as their consultant, have established a $25 million fund to promote the availability of services and improve their quality. This consortium claims to have already assisted local not-for-profit groups in hundreds of locations to establish or improve child care services (Adolf, 1993). One-and-a-half million dollars of this fund have been allocated for the improvement of elder care service availability.

Sick Child Care, Preschool, and After-school Programs

Though day care is the principal service demand of parents in the work force, there has been some growth in the availability of sick-child care services. Fel-Pro in Skokie, Illinois, sends a professional caregiver to the homes of employees to care for sick children, at a cost to the employee of $2 per hour (Fernandez, 1990). Hospitals are among the employers most likely to offer child care assistance. They and other health care vendors see this as a market opportunity for the future.

Another growth area is the preschool and after-school care programs. Connecticut has eight family resource centers operated at public schools which offer full-day preschool and after-school care for children up to age 12. The Connecticut program includes both extended day programs for 3–5-year-old children and for children who are in school. The program is available on a year-round basis (Paul Vivian, Family Resource Centers program manager, personal communication, January 27, 1994). Every public elementary school in Hawaii offers an after-school program, and the state offers full-day kindergarten (The National Report on Work and Family, 1993). A number of school districts, such as Montgomery County, Maryland, have established programs in response to parental demand which are partly subsidized by the school system (using school facilities) and partly supported by fees. In Orange County, California, 11 developers provided funds for local schools to establish after-school child care programs (Fernandez, 1990). Private schools and parish schools also offer these after-school programs. A number of companies sponsor summer day camp, before- and after-school programs, field trips on school holidays, and related programs. The Conference Board (1993) has just completed a report on current corporate practices.

ELDER CARE SERVICES

Adult Day Care Services

There are currently some 2,000 adult day care centers in the
United States, and that number is growing rapidly. Many adult
day care centers are free-standing local not-for-profit organizations. Others are attached to hospitals or nursing homes.
There are also a number of profit day care chains, although
none of the same national scope as companies like Kinder
Care. The average fee for adult day care is about $30 per day,
although there may be significant regional variation. The State
Office on Aging, or the local regional Area Agency on Aging
(found in most communities) can provide complete listings of
adult day care centers in any area of the country. The adult
day care community is organized nationally through the National Council on the Aging (NCOA) in its National Institute
on Adult Day Care.

Long-distance Care and Home Care

Leaders in the service sector, such as Fran Rodgers of Work
Family Directions (Rodgers & Rodgers, 1989), recognize that
elder care is a much more complex arena than child care, and
the number and types of services necessary for the care of
elders can require a variety of forms of expertise that must
be coordinated. Most elderly persons do not live with their
caregivers, and many are at a good distance (Carlson, 1989).
Thus, organizations that can provide home assessment of the
needs of elders and coordinate services may be particularly
valuable to long-distance caregivers, as discussed in Chapter 3.

The National Association of Private Geriatric Care Managers is a rapidly growing association of individual professionals and profit groups who can provide these services.
ANSER (Aging Network Services), based in Bethesda, Maryland, a national organization of geriatric social workers, offers
similar services. Not-for-profit organizations such as the Visiting Nurse Association or Family Service America can also
assess the needs of an elder or assist with care management.

Jewish community and family service agencies have established a national program for such long-distance services. Normal fees for a first-time assessment may run to several hundred dollars, with follow-up care management services priced according to the number of hours per month. Ninety dollars per hour would be an average fee.

EDUCATIONAL PROGRAMS AND
RESOURCE MATERIALS

Educational Programs

Companies may purchase training and educational programs as part of a package with resource and referral or other services. These services may also be purchased separately, however, or may form the primary support program offered to employees. GMAC (General Motor Acceptance Corporation), for example, provides an on-going program of lunch time forums on family issues for employees. This service is provided for GMAC by Initiatives, Inc., a vendor of work–family services based near Horsham, Pennsylvania. Companies may purchase such services through not-for-profit family service agencies, local colleges, or other vendors. Prices may vary from $1,000 per program to a couple of hundred dollars. It may also be possible to arrange for an Area Agency on Aging (AAA) or other public agency to provide some programs for free. In a recent survey of AAAs conducted by the National Association of Area Agencies on Aging (1992), a significant number of respondents reported providing some services at no charge, while others charged a nominal fee.

Resource Materials

Written materials and videos on family care problems are available from a wide variety of sources. The U.S. Department of Labor Women's Bureau sponsors a "Clearinghouse on Work and Family" which provides model program information on work–family issues. The American Association of Retired Persons has prepared a wide assortment of materials on issues affecting the elderly, as have the National Council on the Aging, the American Society on Aging, and such public bodies as the National Institute on Aging (a branch of the National Institutes on Health). Parent Action, the National Council of Jewish Women, and other bodies have materials on child care issues. The Washington Business Group on Health and the New York Business Group on Health are also sources of child or elder care materials, as are vendors of resource and referral services, many consultants and colleges and universities. Mary E. Longe, Deerfield, Michigan, has created Longe Life Libraries as resource centers and family concerns located at the workplace.

CONSORTIA OF COMPANIES AND VENDORS

Chapter 8 will discuss public–private partnerships in depth, but there are many consortia of employers around the nation. Some consortia include both employers and vendors. There are also many vendor organizations. In San Francisco, for example, the United Way initiated "One Small Step" in 1986 to help local employers solve child care problems. The initial group of 15 public and private sector members found that many members were unaware of resources in the community or of programs developed by other companies in the area. Today almost 100 employers are members, and it has expanded its focus to elder care and other work–family issues. One Small Step has opened affiliate membership to vendors of services, labor representatives, university, and other researchers and consultants (David, 1993).

The Metropolitan Washington Council of Governments has established the Work and Family Coalition which meets regularly and sponsors special conferences on work–family issues. The Chicago Metropolitan Work and Family Council, the Alliance of Businesses for Childcare Development (Los Angeles) and the Employer Supported Family Care Network in Boston are examples of similar forums or partnerships in which companies can jointly sponsor specific services, share program ideas and successful models, and inform each other about resources in the community. A recent (January, 1993) meeting of the organizing committee of the National Work Family Alliance noted that employers join organizations such as these in order to gain information. Some members drop out after they have achieved their end (Cramer, personal communication, March 11, 1993).

NATIONAL ORGANIZATIONS

National membership bodies of corporations such as the Conference Board, the New York Business Group on Health, and the Washington Business Group on Health, provide informational materials, research surveys of corporate practice, conferences and other information-sharing vehicles for their memberships. The National Association for Child Care Resource and Referral Agencies, the Association of Child Care Consultants, and a nascent body, the National Work Family Alliance, seek to bring under one umbrella organizations that help businesses implement work–family programs.

A number of groups sponsor annual conferences or similar events that bring together a wide array of business executives, profit and not-for-profit vendors, consultants, and academics. The Conference Board, the Bureau of National Affairs, and other organizations offer opportunities to learn the state of the art from experts and mingle with colleagues from across America.

PUBLIC–PRIVATE PARTNERSHIPS

In recent years, public–private partnerships have become more and more common, as government and industry seek to maximize leverage and reduce unnecessary duplication. In New York City, for example, American Express, Morgan Stanley, and Phillip Morris came together with the New York City Office on Aging to establish the Partnership for Eldercare as a subsidiary of the Office on Aging. The Partnership initially received grants for a several year period from the companies and provided workshops, information, and counseling to employees with elderly relatives. Currently the Partnership has contractual relationships with a number of companies.

A program instruction from the U.S. Administration on Aging (1990) explicitly allowed agencies funded by the Administration on Aging to offer contractual services to companies under specific guidelines which ensure that public services will not be impaired. Today more than 60 Area Agencies on Aging (AAA) act as subcontractors for national vendors of R&R services related to elder care (National Association of Area Agencies on Aging, 1992). Since all AAAs are required to offer information and referrals on aging services to the public, there exists a strong potential for partnership on R&R services. All states also conduct a clearinghouse on child care services.

A myriad of collaborations now occur on the local, state, and national levels and allow executives to find services for employees at lower costs than they would incur by developing their own stand-alone services.

REFERENCES

Adolf, B. P. (1993). Life cycle benefits. *Employee Benefits Journal, 18*(1), 13–20.

Carlson, E. (1989, November 17). Small firms increasingly target market for parent care. New York: *Wall Street Journal*, Enterprise Column.

Conference Board. (1993). *Work family roundtable: School-age programs*. New York: Author.

Conference Board. (1991). *The emerging role of the work-family manager* (Report No. 987). New York: Author.

David, J. (1993, January). *1993 Affiliate Directory*. San Francisco, CA: One Small Step, Inc.

Fernandez, J. P. (1990). *The politics and reality of family care in corporate America*. Lexington, MA: Lexington Books.

Freudenheim, M. (1992, May 8). IBM forms company to sell employee benefit services. New York: *New York Times*, p. D5.

Health Action Forum of Greater Boston. (1989). *Directory of providers offering eldercare services to corporations in eastern Massachusetts*. Boston, MA: Author.

National Association of Area Agencies on Aging. (1992). *Corporate eldercare: The aging network's response to the needs of employed caregivers*. Washington, DC: Author.

The National Report on Work and Family. (1993, February), 6, 4. Silver Spring, MD: Business Publishers.

Rosenzweig, S. & Kramer, E. P. (1992). Human Resources: Get with the program. *Small Business Reports, 17*(8), 20–24.

Smith, D. M. (1991). *Kincare and the American corporation*. Homewood, IL: Business One Irwin.

Rodgers, F. S., & Rodgers, C. (1989). Business and the facts of family life. *Harvard Business Review, 67*(6), 121–129.

U.S. Administration on Aging. (1990). *Program instruction to state and area agencies on aging administering plans under Title III of the Older Americans Act of 1965, as amended* (AOA Pl-90-06). Washington, DC: Author.

7 Union–Management Relations and Family Issues

Historically labor–management relations have been adversarial. Over the years, however, there have been significant examples of collaboration between unions and management. An important area of such collaboration has been the work and family arena. The recent contract negotiated between the Communications Workers of America and the International Brotherhood of Electrical Workers and AT&T provides for a national community-based Child Care Resource and Referral Service engaged by the company to help employees find quality child care, and a similar service for the elder care needs of full-time and part-time employees. (AFL-CIO, 1992). The agreements with AT&T as well as a number of other companies in the communications field are outstanding illustrations of this sort of collaboration. Indeed they suggest that unions and management can work as partners in particular circumstances.

American unions have responded in a variety of ways to the needs of their members. Today the concerns of the labor movement have extended beyond the bargaining table to a belief in labor's responsibility to enhance the overall quality of life for working people. As noted in the chapter on employee assistance programs, some unions have established an analogous program—the Member Assistance Program—which performs similar counseling functions for members. Another approach to assisting union members is a mutual assistance program among active members and retirees of the International Ladies' Garment Workers' Union (ILGWU). Teamsters Local 237 in New York City has established educational and assistance programs for the elder care needs of retirees. International unions and locals throughout the United States have been responsible for specific workplace programs and policies achieved through collective bargaining, as well as the development of union sponsored service programs. In the legislative arena, labor took a strong affirmative position during the long battle to pass the Family and Medical Leave Act.

STATEMENTS AND RESOLUTIONS

There have been important statements of policy and program direction from leadership bodies in the labor movement in the last few years. These statements have articulated a strong positive stance towards the family concerns of workers and provide a rationale for collective bargaining on work–family issues and for lobbying efforts on behalf of specific pieces of legislation such as the Family and Medical Leave Act. The discussion of such statements and policy positions here is, of course, limited in nature and seeks only to cite some of the key statements.

The AFL-CIO Executive Council issued a Statement on Work and Family at the annual conference in 1986 in which it urged Congress to "pass legislation to ensure that parents can take a reasonable parental leave to care for newborn, newly adopted or seriously ill children without risking loss of their jobs" and urged affiliates to "pursue family-strengthening programs through collective bargaining, including joint employer–union sponsored day care centers, information and referral services, allowances for care in existing centers, time off when the child or dependent is sick, and flexible working hours to accommodate caring for children or other dependents" (AFL-CIO, Working Family Resource Guide, 1992, p. 47). The AFL-CIO guide incorporates the full text of that statement as well as several more recent statements and resolutions by individual unions.

The American Federation of State, County, and Municipal Employees (AFSCME) issued a statement on caregivers for the aging in 1990 which noted that more than half of the caregivers for the elderly are also participants in the work force. It resolved to encourage employers to assist caregivers through leave policies, on-site day care, flexible work schedules and job sharing, information and referral services, workshops, counseling, and other responses. The AFSCME also resolved to promote state and federal legislation to aid family caregivers, including unpaid job leave and a federal social insurance program to cover the cost of long-term care.

The 1990 statement by AFSCME on child care resolved to push for a comprehensive federal child care bill and to urge increased federal funding for Head Start and the Child Care Food Program. It encouraged district councils and locals to conduct a needs assessment survey of members regarding family needs including care for elders or other relatives. If such needs are identified, the local should work to establish child care or elder care programs through collective bargaining, labor–management committees, state and federal legislation initiatives, and through coalitions of community groups, not-for-profit providers, unions, and others.

In 1985 the Coalition of Labor Union Women (CLUW) published *Bargaining for Child Care: Contract Language for Union Parents*. The contract language proposed in that document provided the basis for negotiations on child care issues in the late 80s and contributed to the education of advocacy groups, government agencies, bargaining teams, and others. However, following this publication, the rapid evolution of the work and family arena and the development of clauses in labor–management agreements led to a more detailed agenda of work and family concerns within a very few years. The result of this rapid evolution was the publication of a manual for negotiation of family benefits, *Bargaining for Family Benefits: A Union Member's Guide* by the Coalition of Labor Union Women, in 1991. This was followed in 1992 by the *AFL-CIO Working Family Resource Guide: Putting Families First*.

In the Message from Lane Kirkland (AFL-CIO president) and Joyce Miller (CLUW president) that prefaces *Putting Families First*, these leaders cite the tremendous growth in women's labor force participation, the escalating divorce rate, and the increasing number of single parent families as major factors

affecting the workplace and family structure which call for
response from the major institutions of society. The AFL-CIO
(1992) text states in the introduction, "Unions have special
responsibilities and opportunities to promote and defend family-oriented programs, both public and private, and to pursue family-strengthening programs through the collective
bargaining process" (p. 1).

The publication of such documents provides both the
mandate and some tools for collective bargaining on family
issues. Yet it is striking that these leadership statements focus on public policies and collective bargaining almost exclu-
sively. They acknowledge the need for community outreach
and for joint action with other organizations, but they advert
little to the internal support that unions can offer their membership in their struggles to meet both work and family obligations. However, when unions are seen to be genuinely engaged in family issues affecting members, their engagement
can have dramatic effects in such areas as recruitment of new
members and member involvement with the union (*Bargaining for Family Benefits*, 1991).

CURRENT UNION EFFORTS

There have been a wide range of projects undertaken by unions
in the work–family arena. In this section two projects are highlighted: one, an internal support program for retirees by retirees, the other, an innovative training program.

The International Ladies' Garment Workers' Union (ILGWU)
in 1967 developed the Friendly Visitor Program in which retirees visit retirees. Each ILGWU retiree receives a "friendly
visitor" within a year of retirement. After that visit retirees
automatically receive a visit once every two years until age
80. After 80, visits occur every year. If problems in living are
found and a retiree needs help, the friendly visitor alerts the
Retiree Service Department in New York and helps in whatever way possible. The 140,000 ILGWU retirees are found
mostly in New York, New Jersey, the New England states,
Florida, and California. Friendly visitors help with government
and union benefits and services, and they help retirees take

advantage of local resources, also. Friendly visitors are trained through an initial orientation. They attend monthly meetings with a social work supervisor and small group meetings with fellow visitors (Wineman, 1990, Winter).

The New York City Labor Council recognized the need for elder care awareness building among union negotiators and other staff. In response to this need, the NYC Labor Council, in collaboration with the Brookdale Center on Aging at Hunter College, developed an innovative approach to awareness building regarding elder care. A special module on elder care was developed and included in the section on workplace stress in a pre-existing Peer Counseling Training Program. The peer counseling program trains members to identify and respond to substance abuse problems among union members. Participants in the peer counseling program receive credit towards a counseling certificate, so participation is high. The Eldercare Module presented elder care as another workplace stress of which counselors should be aware. The module was very well received and generated a lot of interest in elder care issues among the participants. This NYC Central Labor Council program is an easily replicated model of a way to assist smaller unions to respond to such issues (N. True, personal communication, July 13, 1993).

The above examples illustrate the capabilities of unions to develop effective internal support programs in the work–family area. However, the recession in the United States in recent years, combined with the escalation of health costs and the corporate effort to control such costs, may make it very difficult for union leaders to focus on issues beyond job retention and health care.

In a recent analysis of 452 labor–management agreements in place on July 1, 1990, or later, approximately 50% had one or more conventional work and family provisions (defined in the next paragraph) covering more than two thirds of the workers in the study. Such provisions were much more likely in manufacturing than in services, where only one third of workers had conventional work and family provisions. Work and family provisions were particularly absent from agreements in the construction industry. The short-term nature of projects in that industry was cited as the primary reason for this shortfall, though one might also surmise a connection to the fact that the construction industry is male dominated. Forty unions had one or more contracts with work–family provisions, and eight unions had at least 10 agreements with them. These unions were the International Brotherhood of Electrical Workers, the Food and Commercial Workers, the Steelworkers, the Teamsters, the Clothing and Textile Workers, the Machinists, and the Communications Workers of America. These eight unions represent 62% of the 227 agreements with work and family provisions (Bureau of Labor Management Relations, 1992). The analysis by the Bureau, which excluded public sector agreements and had other limitations of scope, found that the majority of union responses to family issues in its study cohort have come from only eight unions. The unions involved, however, are powerful leaders in the union movement.

The study defined three categories of work and family clauses. First were clauses specifically concerned with conventional areas of interest, including maternity and parental leave, adoptions, child care, elder care, leave for family illness, and employee assistance programs. Second were clauses open to interpretation by the parties to accommodate family needs, including compressed work weeks, personal and sick leaves, flexible schedules, personal and floating holidays, and vacations in daily increments or less. The third category included miscellaneous clauses touching on matters affecting the family, especially those involving family finances (personal financial planning, group insurance programs, mortgage allowances, employee purchases and discounts, and tuition assistance and parental loan programs).

The "Labor Month in Review" column in the *Monthly Labor Review* (1992) notes that work–family issues were not central to labor relations in the 70s and 80s. Thus, responses to these issues were adopted piecemeal into agreements and added to existing clauses. Maternity and paternal leave were added to the existing leave clauses and pay for maternity leave was added to the sickness and accident section of the health benefits clause. This practice led to the scattering of work and family issues throughout agreements.

Recently, negotiators in the telephone industry and elsewhere have begun to concentrate work and family provisions in one place in bargaining agreements. This reflects a recognition that work and family issues have achieved a status of importance for at least some sectors of the labor force. As *Bargaining for Family Benefits: A Union Member's Guide* (1991) put it, "Unions everywhere are, more and more, making family issues a top priority" (p. ix). That statement must, however, be placed in the sobering context of the Bureau of Labor Management's research study, and we must recognize that, while much has been achieved, only half of the agreements in that study had any explicit work–family provisions.

THE CANADIAN EXPERIENCE

In December, 1983, the Canadian Auto Workers (CAW) negotiated the inclusion of a day care fund in the union contract with Canadian Fab, an American Motors subsidiary. This was the first private-sector union contract in Canada to include a day care fund, (*Work and Family: The Crucial Balance*, 1992). Though the original goal of that fund was to establish a day care center, barriers, such as the lack of an appropriate space, prevented reaching this goal. Currently the fund assists workers in paying fees at local day care centers.

In the spring of 1987, the CAW surveyed its membership prior to negotiations with Ford, Chrysler, and GM. The need for child care was recognized along with the fact that age demographics would cause a high turnover of employees in the next decade. The new employees would be younger and a higher proportion would need day care. In the subsequent national collective agreement in September, 1987, a $1.5 million fund was established, a consultant on day care was hired, and a group day care center was opened in November, 1989, in the Windsor-Essex of Ontario area as a model pilot program.

The CAW has established a model for on-site child care for members attending the union's Family Education Center in Port Elgin, Ontario. The union has also established many family-oriented programs for its membership, including a comprehensive legal services plan, union counseling, and substance abuse initiatives. Robert White, of the CAW, regarded as one of the foremost union leaders in Canada, describes some of the CAW programs in "Changing Needs of Work and Family: A Union Response," in the *Canadian Business Review* (1989).

However, the CAW is not alone in developing child care programs. Even workplaces with a small number of employees have responded to collective bargaining. For example, the YWCA of Metro Toronto and the Federation of Community Agency Groups' (CUPE) contract provides a monthly payment of $50 per month for the first child under 12 and $20 per month for each additional child; the payments offset child care costs. The YWCA also has a very flexible work-hours program (number of days per week and hours per day are flexible), and this is fully supported by the union (*Work and Family: The Crucial Balance*, 1992).

A number of unions have established collective agreements which include family-supportive arrangements, and the Ontario Federation of Labor at its annual convention in 1989 issued a statement on families which recognized that family and work was an important labor issue. Robert White, leader of the Canadian Automobile Workers union, articulated these concerns also in an article on "Changing Needs of Work and Family: A Union Response" (1989). The document set out a program for implementation by affiliates and stated that affiliates should continue to make quality issues a negotiating priority. Indeed, *Work and Family: The Crucial Balance* (1992) states, "Employers should expect to see more work and family issues brought to the bargaining table and written into collective agreements. Clearly, the potential exists for greater cooperation between business and labour in the development of family-supportive programs and initiatives" (p. 25).

One may summarize the evolution of collective bargaining in the work–family arena by saying that there has been a steady growth in awareness of these concerns. Major unions have negotiated specific work–family clauses in their agreements with companies over the last few years. The Coalition of Labor Union Women and the AFL-CIO have published important guides for future directions. In Canada, the Ontario Federation of Labour has also issued a clear policy statement and program agenda. Senior union leaders in both countries, such as Lane Kirkland of the AFL-CIO and Robert White of the CAW, have made strong statements of support for a union-based family agenda in the 1990s.

INTERNAL UNION RESPONSES

Establishing A Work and Family Committee

The first step in developing a union response to work and family concerns, according to the CLUW publication, *Bargaining for Family Benefits*, is the establishment of a work and family committee. The book goes on to offer the model developed by the Oil, Chemical and Atomic Workers, Local 8-149 (May & Dudzic, 1990):

- Membership is made up of rank and file members.
- The committee seeks to build an alliance between workers, their families and the community.
- The committee seeks to become a permanent union component.
- The committee is recognized through negotiations as the union group which deals with the employer on family issues.
- It establishes a long-range strategy with achievable goals.
- It speaks for the family concerns of all union members.

Programs developed by the Committee on Work and Family fall into three categories:

1. Changing company policies or developing new ones. This task is undertaken primarily through collective bargaining.
2. Community outreach to publicize issues, find resources and advocate improvements in community services. Grouped with this category would be legislative advocacy.
3. Self-help activities that union members can initiate and carry out themselves, such as establishment of an emergency child care network among parents at a work site.

The CLUW document suggests that a work and family committee raise family issues at union meetings, get work–family stories into union newsletters, advocate for inclusion of family members at union events, and arrange for child care at union meetings. There is no information available as we go to press regarding the prevalence of work–family committees among United States unions, but it seems likely to become a recognized component of most unions in the near future.

Finding the Facts

Before initiating any specific bargaining goal, the work and family committee needs to know the real needs and wants of union members and their families. A needs assessment survey is recommended by CLUW as the best means to achieve this goal, and *Bargaining for Family Benefits: A Union Member's Guide* (1991) provides two sample survey questionnaires. Different methods for ensuring a good response rate are offered, from a special union meeting to fill out the questionnaire, to distribution through stewards. Since survey response rates can vary a great deal, it is important that advance publicity be undertaken and that follow-up be undertaken, also, either by stewards or by committee members, to ensure the maximum possible response. If response rates are low, it becomes very hard to assume that the survey tells us the real needs of all union members. Dr. Margaret Neal (personal communication, June 23, 1993) recently confirmed the necessity for good advance publicity and endorsement from senior corporate executives in workplace surveys. By extension, the committee on work and family may want to obtain a strong endorsement from the local president. Confidentiality may be just as important for the union member as it is when employees respond to a similar corporate questionnaire. Anonymity can be ensured by having an outside consultant or faculty from a local college analyze the data. Perhaps responses can be sealed before return, or can be mailed directly to the outside body. A careful approach can result in a high response rate, and will provide information which can buttress union bargaining positions.

A needs survey can ensure that the work and family committee is truly responsive to the real concerns of members and their families. Mindy Fried, (1987) in *Babies and Bargaining*, provides an example of a union local in California which wanted to bargain with Santa Clara County for an on-site child care center. However, a survey of members found that their biggest concern was for care of children before and after school. The union then negotiated the organization of a joint union–county child care committee to meet and confer regarding establishment of a child care program for county workers at no cost to the county. The result was a creative collaboration between the school district, the workers, and the YWCA, which was quite different from the initial on-site day care center idea, but met the needs of more union members. Because surveys are sometimes regarded as unnecessary and time consuming it is heartening to note that the AFSCME formally encouraged its councils and locals to undertake surveys of members in its 1990 Statement on Child Care (*AFL-CIO Working Family Resource Guide*, 1992, p. 62).

There have been a large number of surveys conducted on a national basis, for example, the American Association of Retired Persons' 1989 survey of working caregivers, or within specific companies, such as the Travelers Insurance Company's pioneering 1985 survey of its employees on elder care.

The mandate for union involvement contained in those studies has been implicit in the chapter on demographic issues (see Chapter 1). A major factor is alluded to in the introduction to *Bargaining for Family Benefits* (1991), namely the rapid growth in female participation in the work force. The authors point out that Department of Labor data indicate that, between 1990 and 1995, women will fill two-thirds of new jobs. They further point out that most of these women will have babies at some time during their working lives and will return to work before the baby's first birthday (p. xi). The Canadian perspective on labor force change emphasizes: a) An increase in the number of dual-career families, b) more heads of single-parent families, c) more women of all ages and at all stages of their lives, d) a greater proportion of women with children, particularly mothers of young children, e) more men with direct responsibility for family care, f) growing numbers of workers caring for elderly parents and relatives, and g) an increase in the number of workers caring for persons with disabilities (*Work and Family: The Crucial Balance*, 1992).

While particular unions may be affected more or less by the trends described above, it is obviously important to assess the needs of union members from their own perspectives, and surveys of work–family issues can be conducted by the union internally or through the workplace in cooperation with management. Those needs will also be affected by the availability of services in the local community. If there is no affordable day care for children, then affordable day care is highly likely to be an area of need in a local with many young members. Similarly, the availability of public transportation may be a critical issue for members responsible for the care of elders; or the most urgent need may be for an after-school program for latch key children.

Outreach to the Community

The primary emphasis in union resolutions, statements, and other documents, is on contract negotiations with employers regarding work conditions and family related benefits. There is also a strong emphasis on legislative advocacy and some emphasis on community outreach.

Community outreach is obviously important in assessing the resources available to caregiving union members. Likewise, outreach can bring together not-for-profit service providers, churches and synagogues, schools, and other interested parties, to develop services which can meet the needs of others in the community besides the union members. In some cases, the union is a party to a labor agreement which provides some resources to help communities develop child care and elder care services. For example, the 1990 contract between AT&T and the Communications Workers of America and the International Brotherhood of Electrical Workers specifically includes a $5 million fund for center development (Scott, 1990). Clearly that fund is not capable of supporting the development of many centers without local community participation.

In other cases, the union work and family committee or designated group can act as a catalyst in brokering a community agreement. The Santa Clara County/SEIU (Service Employees International Union) joint committee brokered a relationship between parents in need of an after-school program for children with the needs of a community school system facing falling enrollment and, hence, falling budget resources. Parents from outside who worked in the county enrolled their children in Santa Clara in return for an after-school program at one school. The YWCA administers the program (*Bargaining for Family Benefits*, 1991).

In short, union members, through their work and family committees, can research the resources available to meet the needs of members with family responsibilities. They can identify the gaps in services and the groups or organizations with an interest in meeting those needs or contributing resources to the effort. Corporate executives can contribute much to the solution of work–family problems; however, they may live in very different circumstances from line workers and may have little concept of the caregiving resources or deficits in some communities. Union members are likely to be more aware of the specific situation in their own neighborhoods. The cooperation of union leadership is also vital to the success of rank and file initiatives.

JOINT LABOR–MANAGEMENT PROJECTS

Joint labor–management responses to work–family issues have been established through contract negotiations in a number of companies, public agencies, and not-for-profit institutions. CLUW suggests that "an important first step at the bargaining table may be the establishment of a labor-management committee on family issues" (*Bargaining for Family Benefits*, 1991, p. 7). Such a step is not regarded as a cost by companies; it can help establish the basis for action if the employer is genuinely interested, and at least a forum for issues if not. CLUW urges that contract language specify who is responsible for tasks, when each action is to start and conclude, how committee costs will be paid, and what other financial commitment the employer is willing to make at the start. Labor–management committees have initiated employee surveys on family issues, assessed community resources, helped establish company policies to assist working caregivers, and undertaken other activities.

Other accomplishments achieved by unions include union sponsored or jointly sponsored day care centers. The ILGWU Chinatown Child Care Center in New York City is co-sponsored by the city and the trade association for the garment industry, along with the union. The Merrimack River Child Care Center in Lawrence, Massachusetts, was funded by an employer, union member contributions, the city of Lawrence, and state subsidies from the State of Massachusetts. Before- and after-school programs for latch key children, emergency and sick child care, and information and referral services, are further examples of support programs established through union negotiation.

SUMMARY

Unions have clearly recognized family issues as an important part of the union agenda over the past decade. From resolutions and statements, to specific contract agreements and the proliferation of work–family committees, to the more recent development of benefits negotiation guides, there has been a consistent progression in union response to work–family concerns. Nonetheless, many unions have not moved work–family concerns to the foreground of their bargaining efforts, and the current recession may contribute to further delay.

Unions traditionally recognize and bring to the bargaining table the real concerns of workers. They have the capacity to act as a catalyst, bringing together employers, community agencies, and voluntary groups in innovative and truly communal responses. They also have the capacity to provide internal support systems, member to member, and through such support systems as member assistance programs and retiree service programs. This can result in a significant contribution to the daily capacity of workers to cope with working and caregiving.

The proliferation of work and family committees will enable labor to further the goal of enhancement of the overall quality of the lives of union members. They can be the stepping stone to a new generation of internal union programs which will express the true spirit of "union."

REFERENCES

AFL-CIO working family resource guide: Putting families first. (1992). Washington, DC: The AFL-CIO Department of Employee Benefits.

Bureau of Labor Management Relations. (1992). *Work and family provisions in major collective bargaining agreements* (Report No. 144). Washington, DC: Author.

Bargaining for child care: Contract language for union parents. (1985). New York: Coalition of Labor Union Women.

Bargaining for family benefits: A union member's guide. (1991). New York: Coalition of Labor Union Women.

Fried, M. (1987). *Babies and bargaining.* Southeastern, MA: Labor Education Center.

Labor Month in Review. (1992). *Monthly Labor Review, 115*(6), 2.

May, L., & Dudzic, M. (1990). *Building work and family committees: A union based approach.* Rahway, NJ: Oil, Chemical and Atomic Workers, Local 8–149.

Work and family: The crucial balance. (1992). Toronto: The Ministry of Community and Social Services, Ontario Women's Directorate.

Scott, M. B. (1990, May). How companies help with family care. *Employee Benefit Plan Review, 15,* 12–29.

White, R. (1989). Changing needs of work and family: A union response. *Canadian Business Review,* 19 (Autumn), 32.

Wineman, J. (1990, Winter). Friendly visitors reach out to retirees. *Together on Aging,* pp. 3, 8. Washington, DC: Washington Business Group on Health.

8 Public–Private Partnerships in Work–Family Services

There are a wide variety of public–private partnerships in the effort to meet the needs of employee caregivers in America. Such collaboration has been inherent in the structure of bodies like the United Way of America, which raises some three billion dollars each year (primarily through corporate and public sector workplace campaigns) to support a wide range of community service agencies. On a smaller scale, corporations have sponsored or assisted a multitude of local service agencies throughout the modern era.

THE AMERICAN BUSINESS COLLABORATION

Perhaps the best known effort to explicitly assist family support services is the American Business Collaboration for Quality Dependent Care. Currently 146 businesses and other organizations are participating in the project, which has a total of $26.1 million in corporate funds available to assist local groups around the nation as of April, 1993 (*The National Report on Work and Family*, 1993a). Among the 300 projects which have been assisted through the fund and the Work Family Directions Development Corporation, the project consultant, are a child care center expansion in Poughkeepsie, New York, sponsored by the Culinary Institute of America, IBM, Marist College, Saint Francis Hospital, Vassar Brothers Hospital, and Vassar College; a training course for child care centers in Denver, sponsored by IBM, Travelers, and AT&T; and a family day care accreditation project in Raleigh/ Durham, funded by GLAXCO and IBM which is helping 18 family day care providers to become accredited by the National Association for Family Day Care.

PUBLIC AGENCIES SEEK PARTNERSHIPS

In recent years, public agencies have also entered into explicit collaboration or contractual relationships with companies. The New York City Office on Aging has been a leader in this area. It established a multi-year partnership with several major corporations, including American Express and J.P. Morgan Bank. The partnership allowed the Office on Aging to establish a subsidiary which provides education, counseling, and information and referral (I&R) services to an array of more than 35 companies (Garrison & Jelin, 1990).

In 1990, the U.S. Administration on Aging issued a program instruction on the subject of corporate elder care. The instruction (U.S. Administration on Aging, 1990) encouraged state and area agencies on aging to be in the forefront of engagement with the private sector, provided always that such relations conform with both the letter and the spirit of the Older Americans Act. The book, *Corporate Eldercare: The Aging Network's Response To The Needs of Employed Caregivers*, (National Association of Area Agencies on Aging, 1992) reports on a 1989 survey of Area Agencies on Aging (AAAs) and found that 112 AAAs were providing some elder care services to employers at that time, although most services were provided gratis. Some 27 AAAs reported an ongoing contractual relationship with employers at that time. A later national survey in 1991 found that 84 AAAs were providing education, I&R, and/or case management services to employers. One hundred and seventy-eight AAAs reported providing or offering training, retirement planning, needs assessment, and caregiver support services. It was notable that the total response to the 1989 survey was 120 AAAs while 419 responded to the 1991 survey (National Association of Area Agencies on Aging, 1992). The great increase in the number of responding agencies suggests that awareness of public–private partnership options has grown quite rapidly among these agencies in a very few years. However, it must also be noted that 39% of AAAs did not respond to the survey, presumably because they were not involved with corporate elder care issues at that time.

NATIONAL STUDIES OF
PUBLIC–PRIVATE PARTNERSHIPS

The General Accounting Office (GAO), in response to congressional queries, has undertaken several studies of issues related to corporate contracting with Area Agencies on Aging (AAAs). Two of these studies have been released at the time of writing while two further studies are still underway. The GAO studies are the first research based evaluations of public–private partnerships in the work–family arena to our knowledge, and they certainly can be regarded as the most comprehensive effort to date; however, they are limited to the elder care sector. On July 7, 1992, a report was released on state agencies on aging policies regarding elder care. In 1990, the U.S. Administration on Aging (AoA) asked state agencies to develop policies in this area. The study examined whether the states had established policies which permit elder care contracts. The study also assessed whether these policies ensured that their public mission would be preserved when AAAs enter corporate elder care contracts (U.S. General Accounting Office, 1992).

The GAO study found that 45 states and the District of Columbia have developed policies which permit, and in many cases encourage, AAAs to enter corporate elder care contracts. (The states of Delaware, Alaska, New Hampshire, North Dakota, and South Dakota have established policies stating that they will not enter into contracts with corporations for elder care.) However, 42 of these policies were considered to be inadequate in addressing key issues in the AoA program instruction. Two points were singled out: a) Many states do not provide adequate guidance for ensuring that AoA funded services will be targeted to individuals in greatest economic and social need, and b) many states do not specify that corporate contracts should not restrict the ability of state agencies to oversee area agencies or prevent state agencies from getting the information they need to carry out these responsibilities.

The GAO report suggested that Congress might consider amending the Older Americans Act to clarify the authority of the Administration on Aging to oversee state and AAA activities in corporate elder care partnerships and "to define the agencies' responsibilities for ensuring preservation of public-mission objectives when engaged in such activities" (U.S. General Accounting Office, 1992, p. 9).

This GAO report is undoubtedly a significant contribution to public policy discussion regarding public agencies' involvement in direct contracting for service to employees of corporations. In our view it rightly emphasizes the oversight responsibility of federal and state agencies and affirms properly the priority of socioeconomically disadvantaged persons for service with public funds. However, such a priority is not a mandate of corporate human resource policy; rather, many companies wish to assist employee caregivers without regard to their parents' financial or social status. Although companies may offer sliding scale fees for use of an intergenerational day care center (as Stride Rite does [Leibold, 1990]), or offer subsidies for other services on a similar basis, they would not wish to have public priorities mandate priority for employee access to a corporate sponsored benefit.

A second GAO report, *Older Americans Act: Eldercare Public–Private Partnerships*, was published on April 16, 1993 (U.S. General Accounting Office, 1993). This report contains the results of a survey of 635 of the total 655 Area Agencies on Aging (AAAs) in the USA (five other AAAs are found in Puerto Rico, Guam, and other locations). The study found that for 31 AAAs reporting both cost and income data for elder care services provided in 1991 there was a median profit of $0. Fifteen showed net profit, 13 broke even and 3 reported net losses. The median income generated in 1991 among 56 AAAs reporting data on contracts to provide enhanced information and referral services (that is, service which included at least some level of consultation or counseling) was $660. The report noted that 88% of the 75 AAAs in public–private partnerships provided services to employers through a vendor, and all 66 agencies were associated with three vendors: Work Family Directions, The Partnership Group, or Working Solutions. Five agencies have direct contracts with companies and four have contracts with both companies and vendors.

This report makes it clear that AAAs are not generating any significant income at this time from corporate elder care ventures. However, the report does not contrast the level of income of AAAs providing direct service to companies versus those provided through national vendors. Neither does the report address the potential for future revenues of such direct service or vendor brokered service, nor does it attempt to compare AAA results with the income generated by not-for-profit agencies such as family service agencies.

As noted in Chapter 6, a small number of national vendors seem to dominate the market for service to national or regional corporations. These vendors are generally privately held companies that seem to be very viable and are growing rapidly. It is unlikely that they would do so unless they were generating significant income. Hence, the data available from the GAO suggest that either the vendors—the middle people—are successfully maintaining low reimbursement rates to local agencies, (normally paid on a fee-for-service basis) or the agencies are not pricing their services at sufficient rates to allow a margin of profit.

The purview of the GAO report was not such that marketing efforts could be evaluated, nor was there any estimate of the potential market for corporate elder care services. In the private sector, economies of scale are often realized as the service volume increases. There may be an opportunity of this kind available to AAAs, also, as the demand for service under corporate contracts increases.

Given these limitations, the study remains the only one known to the authors which provides national data on public–private partnerships. It certainly suggests that such partnerships are unlikely to become major revenue enhancers for public agencies. Corporate contracts are unlikely in the current circumstances to provide resources for additional public services. The GAO findings may also indicate a strong need for assistance to AAAs in both marketing and pricing of services.

THE ROLE OF NATIONAL VENDORS

An important factor in the growth of public–private partnerships has been the emergence of national vendors of work–family services (see Chapter 6). The national vendors—such as Work Family Directions, The Partnership Group, Initiatives, Inc., Working Solutions, and Family Service America—typically contract with companies to provide child care resource and referral (R&R) and/or elder care information and referral (I&R) to employees throughout the nation. Training for managers, support group leadership, counseling employees, lunch time forum presentation, and information through handbooks and newsletters may be other services provided.

In most R&R or I&R cases, the vendor subcontracts with not-for-profit agencies throughout the country to provide the local service or information needed. Work Family Directions, for example, currently has some 200 subcontractors for elder care alone. Thus the national vendors of I&R/R&R are highly dependent on local not-for-profit service agencies if they wish to provide quality resources to employees.

As noted above, these vendors seem to be reimbursing local service agencies at a very modest level, sufficient only to cover the cost of the service. National associations such as the National Association of Area Agencies on Aging (with more than 600 AAAs) or the National Association of Child Care Resource and Referral Agencies (600 member agencies, more than 500 R&R agencies) could potentially negotiate with the national vendors on behalf of local service agencies or AAAs and seek higher reimbursement rates for their member agencies. However, no such effort is underway at this time. Perhaps the closest example is Family Service America, which vends the services of its member agencies, and thus has an incentive to share at least some of the profits realized with its member agencies.

CREATIVE COLLABORATION

Creative collaborations between public agencies, not-for-profit service providers, and corporations are springing up in many parts of the country, a number of them supported by the American Business Collaborative. Office park developers now regard the availability of child care at the park an important selling point. Local agencies are invited to provide the service in a space allocated for the purpose. Perhaps the best known example of corporate–public–not-for-profit collaboration is the Stride Rite Intergenerational Day Care Center at the company headquarters in Cambridge, Massachusetts (Leibold, 1990). Stride Rite established a child care center for employees and local community residents in 1971. In 1987–88, the company began plans to expand the facility to an intergenerational care center. The collaborating bodies were the Area Agency on Aging, Stride Rite, and Wellesley College. Wellesley students use the site as a field placement in their curriculum on human development. The Area Agency was able to expand the day care resources available to elders, and the company was able to offer an expanded support service to employees and the local community. Currently, there are some 50 child care spaces and 25 senior spaces available at the center. Employees of Stride Rite can use the facility with a substantial corporate subsidy; other users are provided access on a sliding-scale fee basis. There are several hundred intergenerational day care programs now in operation throughout the United States, according to Generations United research (T. Scannell, personal communication, January 5, 1992). A number of them are located at hospitals and other health care facilities.

The San Francisco Airport Child Care Center is an example of a child care consortium. The center serves employees from 300 businesses, 40 labor organizations, and two hospitals near the airport. The project was initiated by the San Mateo Central Labor Council to meet the needs of shift workers at the airport and local businesses. The not-for-profit organization has a board with representatives of labor groups, corporations, and two counties. San Mateo County paid $1.4 million for the building; the San Francisco Airport Commission financed the construction and remodeling; Mills Peninsula Hospital gave a start-up grant; and United Airlines gave a substantial donation (*The National Report on Work and Family*, 1993b). This is a good example of labor, management, not-for-profit, and public agency collaboration.

THE ROLE OF ADVOCATES

In June of 1993 The Children's Defense Fund published *Investing in Our Children's Care*. The author, Helen Blank (1993), states in the executive summary that "the inadequacy of federal child care funding for low-income working families has been exacerbated in many states by state budget cuts and shortfalls" (p. ix). She concludes that there is urgent need for additional resources from federal, state, and local government, along with corporate, religious, and voluntary organizations, to meet the child care needs of American families. Blank specifically addresses public–private partnerships and states again the necessity for states, local communities, and child care programs to generate private sector resources to bolster federal and state child care investments. She notes that Oregon has supplemented block grant funded work with corporate funds focused on provider recruitment, training, and retention, and now has more than one million dollars in corporate funds. Washington state created a facilities grant fund which provides loans and grants for child care facilities where there is some type of corporate partnership. Michigan requires applicants for its training grants to show how they would use funds to create a public–private partnership.

Ellen Galinsky and associates pointed out in 1991 that an estimated 5,600 companies, out of 6 million nationally, provided employees some form of child care assistance. This represents a 500% increase since 1978 (Galinsky, Friedman & Hernandez, 1991). The number, of course, represents a very small minority of companies, even though the employers involved include many of the largest corporations in America. The Child Care Action Campaign and the Center for Policy Alternatives (1992) copublished *Investing in the Future: Child Care Financing Options for the Public and Private Sectors*. They state that two of the most popular ways for employers to get involved are through expansion of the supply of child care and improvement of the quality of child care. This document also reviews the use of employer tax credits for child care. As of 1991, 14 states offer such credits, directed mostly at real estate and start-up costs, which provide dollar-for-dollar tax liability reduction. However, less than 1% of businesses eligible for these credits claim them. Reasons for the low use rate include: a) the incentive is inadequate, b) the incentive should apply to operations as well as construction, c) use of incentives may increase federal tax liability, d) no benefits are available to employers who are already exempt (i.e., not-for-profits). Private sector options proffered include employer tax credits, employer funds and partnerships, investment funds, bank loans, community development corporations, and pension fund investments.

What is striking about these arrangements, generated mainly by advocacy organizations, is the strong endorsement of public–private partnerships contained in them. Clearly, child care-oriented organizations have adopted a very positive attitude toward corporate involvement in dependent care issues; indeed, no critical or negative stances were found in the child care literature reviewed for this chapter. This attitude is in some contrast to the concerns (accountability issues, responsiveness to public priorities, and very meager financial returns) expressed in the GAO reports on elder care contracts between public agencies (AAAs) and the private sector. Furthermore, the documents reviewed do not provide any guidance on pricing, marketing, or other aspects of doing business with the corporate sector.

CHILD CARE/ELDER CARE PARTNERSHIPS

One of the trends in collaboration is the growing frequency of joint contracting by child care and elder care agencies. Companies today generally include elder care and child care in their dependent care policies and programs. Consequently corporate executives wish to include responses to both needs in their programs. Research findings in Oregon (Neal, Chapman, Ingersoll-Dayton, & Emlen, 1993) and in Fairfax County, Virginia (Fairfax Area Agency on Aging, 1991), affirm that a high proportion of working caregivers have both child and elder care responsibilities simultaneously. As Neal and colleagues note, among the variables in their study of working caregivers, multiple caregiving roles were found to be the most consistent predictor of stress outcomes. They report that such parents "experienced more stress regarding their own health, more caregiving stress regarding their child care arrangements, and more difficulty in combining working with their family responsibilities" (Neal et al., 1993, p. 106). Child care and elder care agencies seeking corporate contracts are therefore coming together with counterpart agencies in order to respond to this corporate agenda. The increasing dialogue and partnership activity among caregiving agencies is likely to produce an ever greater diversity of funding sources for their workplace services: federal, state, corporate, and community, and employee contributions, and user fees.

PUBLIC FINANCING

One should not ignore the tight federal, state, and local budgets for community services when examining the growth of public–private partnerships. The fact is that federal funding for the Older Americans Act services has actually declined since 1981, when adjustment for inflation is made, according to the National Association of Area Agencies on Aging (1994). The Child Care and Development Block Grant program enacted by the federal government in 1990 provided $750 million for FY 1991, $825 million for FY 1992 and $925 million for FY 1993 to states which develop and submit a state plan for the provision of child care services. The Older Americans Act has been supported by some $1.5 billion annually, and the funding levels for child care and development noted above are not insubstantial, but these funding levels are not sufficient to meet the growing needs of children and elders. Thus, Los Angeles County alone estimated that it would need $2.5 billion to meet its child care needs (Fernandez, 1990). When public resources are limited, agencies will reach out for other funding resources such as corporate contracts. Given the current efforts to reduce the federal deficit and the likelihood of substantial deficits into the future, there will continue to be a strong rationale for public and not-for-profit agency efforts to find corporate partners.

PROS AND CONS OF PARTNERING

Corporations also have a rationale for such partnerships. First, the cost of internal child care centers at the workplace may be significantly higher than the cost of collaboration with an existing local day care center. Second, corporate concerns about tort liability can make such outside providers welcome (Fernandez, 1990; Smith, 1991). Third, companies generally desire a "good neighbor" image in the local community and collaboration with local organizations can foster good community relations. Fourth, in an era of corporate downsizing, it makes more sense to contract out for family support services. Fifth, an abundant supply of child and elder care services in the community may make additional internal services redundant.

Partnership arrangements for employees' dependent care needs sometimes fail. In Miami, a church decided that it needed to focus on other ministries and reduce or terminate its commitment to a child care center (Smith, 1991). In Stamford, Connecticut, Champion International initiated a consortium approach to child care, but eventually decided to go it alone after a good deal of time was spent in fruitless negotiation (S. Mullady, personal communication, March 19, 1987). The company culture may also determine corporate strategy in favor of a company service rather than a partnership approach. Dr. Gwen Morgan has found that employers see partnerships as a way to a) offer the best possible service to employees, b) ensure equity in the delivery of services, and c) target services to areas where employees live and work. She also notes that business leaders want private, not governmental, image and promotion of the partnership. In many cases, they also desire confidentiality regarding their employees and monies (Child Care Action Campaign, 1990).

John Fernandez, in his book, *The Politics and Reality of Family Care in Corporate America* (1990), suggests a number of ways in which employers can help employees with child care expenses. One way is to negotiate employee discounts with various types of caregivers and provide subsidies to employees using the service. Employers can provide employees with vouchers to use at their preferred caregiver site or they can purchase a guaranteed number of slots. They can provide in-kind services such as company-owned space; administrative, legal, printing, maintenance or management services; office supplies, equipment or products; low-interest loans for construction or renovation; and payment for staff training at colleges. However, Fernandez recognizes that, relative to the high cost of quality child care, in-kind services are rarely a sufficient contribution (p. 114).

In short, there may be financial, legal, public relations, and employee concerns dictating the direction chosen by a company. Remember too, that *Working Mother*, in an October, 1990, feature on "The 75 Best Companies for Working Mothers," cited data indicating that only 220 corporations, 800 hospitals, and 200 federal and state agencies provided on- or near-site child care in 1990. Similar data on 750 employer-operated day care centers was provided in the Bureau of National Affairs' *82 Key Statistics on Work and Family Issues* (1988). On the other hand, a 1990 survey of its U.S. corporate members by the International Foundation of Employee Benefit Plans (1990) found that employer subsidies for child care expenses are projected to grow rapidly in this decade and reach 52% by the year 2000. Collaboration need not be restricted to child or elder care. Extended-school-day programs can be established by public schools in partnership with employers, for example, the American Bankers Insurance Group (ABIG) collaboration with the Dade County School District, which operates a county public school on company grounds (Smith, 1991).

THE ROLE OF THE STATES

The states vary greatly in their involvement in and support of work–family programs. As noted above, 14 states now offer employer tax credits, and a number of other states are currently considering such programs. Maryland has established the Maryland Child Care Resource Network, a group of corporate, union, foundation, and government leaders, to expand and improve child care. Hawaii has established a model child care program in which participants pay according to the family income and the state subsidizes the balance so that child care providers are paid $350 per child per month. In Washington state, funding for child care has gone from $24 million to $160 million, and the state works closely with employers, encouraging them to offer family-friendly benefits.

Under the California Child Care Initiative, California contributes one dollar for every two dollars raised from private firms, foundations, and community groups to increase the supply of high-quality child care. This plan allows corporations to share the cost of child care with the state and other bodies. While few states are as generous as California, it is obvious that state subsidies and tax credits can enhance corporate interest in partnerships with service agencies in the community.

The Child Care and Development Block Grant Act specifies that 75% of funds be spent on direct services, such as child care or vouchers, and that 25% may be spent for quality enhancement, such as training courses or establishment of clearing houses or offices of child care resource and referral (Blank, 1993). Obviously, the latter use of funds could be of direct benefit to corporate employees or to employee assistance programs, which could utilize a state R&R information service. The states, through their use of block grants, their oversight role regarding public agencies, and regulatory and tax policies, can significantly stimulate or retard public–private partnership activities.

RECIPE FOR SUCCESS

The Child Care Action Campaign (1990) brought a group of corporate leaders, child care advocates, and public officials together for its first national advisory panel exchange. This expert group agreed that the elements critical for a successful public–private venture included the following:

- strong, committed leadership,
- a focus on infrastructure development,
- flexibility,

- a strong community base able to function in different neighborhoods, and
- a network of agencies with child care expertise.

The expert panel also noted that partnerships can pool financial resources, leverage political clout, integrate various perspectives in planning child care service, stimulate greater community awareness about child care, and create a service responsive to all income groups.

The advantages of partnering and the basic requirements suggested here for success seem to apply also to elder care service delivery, or indeed to joint ventures of child and elder care agencies.

SUMMARY

The Children's Defense Fund has recently published a useful review of the use of block grants, *Investing In Our Children's Care: An Analysis of How Block Grant Funds Are Used*, (Blank, 1993). The report notes the limited nature of the funds involved and the wide variety of ways in which states are encouraging public–private collaboration. As discussed earlier, the states vary a good deal in their oversight of public agencies in the elder care arena, five states refusing to participate in corporate contracts and the majority of states encouraging such contracts by area agencies on aging. Thus, limited federal funds and limited corporate support suggest that it may be a long time before the needs of employee caregivers for child care and elder care resources can be fully met. Collaborative ventures and partnerships may become even more attractive if the current climate of scarce resources continues for some time.

In sum, this discussion of public–private collaboration and contracting reveals that a good deal of such activity is underway. There is a growing public sector interest in fostering corporate response to the needs of employee caregivers and in designing collaborative solutions. Companies do not wish to ignore the needs of employees, but find cost sharing prudent today. Not-for-profit agencies and advocacy groups are also eager to join in such ventures.

A cautionary note is necessary, however. Not-for-profit and public agencies need to determine the cost of their services carefully; indeed, they may need bargaining agents, such as national associations, for contract negotiations with national vendors and large corporations. Companies and vendors may also need to pay attention to the public purposes for which public agencies have been established. While public–private collaboration, partnerships, and contractual relationships are now firmly established in the work and family arena, new information technologies, health care reform, and new service providers may transform both the work–family agenda and public–private collaboration as we move through the 1990s.

REFERENCES

Blank, H. (1993). *Investing in our children's care: An analysis of how block grants are used*. Washington, D.C.: The Children's Defense Fund.

Bureau of National Affairs. (1988). *82 key statistics on work & family issues* (Report No. 9). Washington, D.C.: Author.

Child Care Action Campaign. (1990). *Making the connections: Public–private partnerships in child care* (National Advisory Panel Exchange No. 1). New York: Author.

Child Care Action Campaign. (1992). *Investing in the future: Child care financing options for the public and private sectors*. New York: Child Care Action Campaign and The Center for Policy Alternatives.

Fairfax Area Agency on Aging. (1991). *The missing worker: Caring for mom and dad*. Fairfax County, VA: Author.

Fernandez, J. P. (1990). *The politics and reality of family care in corporate America*. Lexington Books, Lexington, MA.

Galinsky, E., Friedman, D. E., & Hernandez, C. A. (1991). *The corporate reference guide to work-family programs*. New York: Families and Work Institute.

Garrison, A., & Jelin, M.A. (1990). *The partnership for eldercare research study*. New York: New York City Department for the Aging.

International Foundation of Employee Benefit Plans. (1990). *Non-traditional benefits for the workforce of 2000*. Brookfield, WI: Author.

Leibold, K. (1990). *Sharing the caring: Options for the 90s and beyond*. In Subcommittee on Human Services, Select Committee on Aging, House of Representatives (Pub. No. 101–750, pp. 20–27). Washington, DC: Government Printing Office.

National Association of Area Agencies on Aging. (1992, April). *Corporate eldercare: The aging network's response to the needs of employed caregivers*. Washington, DC: Author.

National Association of Area Agencies on Aging (1994, January 26). OAA funding trends: Federal dollars adjusted for inflation, graph provided by E. Sheehey, NAAA, Washington, DC.

The National Report on Work and Family. (1993a, April 27). Silver Spring, MD: Business Publishers.

The National Report on Work and Family. (1993b, July 20) 6, Silver Spring, MD: Business Publishers.

Neal, M. B., Chapman, N. J., Ingersoll-Dayton, B., & Emlen, A. C. (1993). *Balancing work and caregiving for children, adults and elders*. Newbury Park, CA: Sage.

Smith, D. M. (1991). *Kincare and the American corporation: Solving the work/family dilemma*. Homewood, IL: Business One Irwin.

The 75 best companies for working mothers. (1990, October). *Working Mother*, 31–64.

U.S. Administration on Aging. (1990). *Program instruction to state and area agencies on aging administering plans under Title III of the Older Americans Act of 1965, as amended. Subject: Eldercare*. (AoA-PL-90-06). Washington, DC: Department of Health and Human Services.

U.S. General Accounting Office. (1992). *Older Americans Act: more federal action needed on public/private partnerships: Report to the Chairman, Subcommittee on Human Services, Select Committee on Aging, House of Representatives*. (GAO/HRD-92-84). Washington DC: Author.

U.S. General Accounting Office. (1993). *Older Americans Act: Eldercare public-private partnerships*. (GAO/PEMD-93-20). Washington DC: Author.

9 Implementing Work and Family Programs in the Workplace

This chapter reviews seven steps frequently taken by unions and workplaces in establishing family-focused workplace programs. Workplace programs include benefits (e.g., family leaves), services (e.g., lunch time seminars), policies (e.g., flextime), and community investments (e.g., grants to child care providers). Steps described here are guidelines subject to modifications by unions and corporations to fit their unique situations. The major steps are:

1. Conducting employee needs assessment
2. Establishing a Work and Family Task Force
3. Developing a strategic plan
4. Implementing program components
5. Marketing the program
6. Training supervisors
7. Evaluating the program

EMPLOYEE NEEDS ASSESSMENT

The purpose of an employee needs assessment is to clarify for the company or union the specific needs of its work force with family responsibilities. The most popular approach is to survey all employees using a self-administered mailed questionnaire. Some companies and unions use in-house staff with expertise in survey techniques to conduct the needs assessment. Scharlach, Lowe, and Schneider (1991) found, however, that use of in-house staff is more costly and time-consuming than often believed. An alternative approach is to hire outside consultants with expertise in work and family programs and in conducting employee needs assessments.

Sample Needs Assessment

A sample needs assessment survey is found in Appendix B. This one is selected because it has been used many times with large and small companies throughout the United States. It also includes all three dependent care groups: children, persons with disabilities, and frail relatives. Finally, it obtains data needed to successfully design work and family programs. The survey includes information on demographics (age, gender, and income); work history (work position, work hours, and work shift); problems with child care, disabled care, and elder care; management practices; work interferences due to dependent care responsibilities; stress (health, job, financial, family relationships); and work and family conflict. We would add a question on ethnicity. Permission to use this survey can be obtained from Arthur Emlen, Professor Emeritus, Portland State University, P.O. Box 751-RRI, Portland, OR 97207.

Fears About Needs Assessments

Companies first thinking about surveying their employees are concerned about employee expectations, equity issues, and corporate expense. The Families and Work Institute found that companies using the survey approach were not bombarded with employee demands for immediate and expensive programs (Galinsky, Friedman, & Hernandez, 1991). Instead, employees responded with appreciation when companies communicated to them that they were concerned about the employee's family commitments and wanted to help them, within reasonable limits.

One way for companies to handle equity issues is to communicate to all employees that the work and family programs are part of a larger concern about worker stress and productivity. Wellness programs as well as work and family programs can be presented as part of this larger perspective. Thus, clear, rational, and thoughtful communication helps the company and employees to see their common concerns and to develop beneficial approaches.

Regarding the expense of conducting an employee needs assessment, companies and unions must weigh the costs against the benefits. The needs assessment helps decision makers design programs that are best suited for each workplace population. Well-conceived programs are more likely to be utilized and to achieve program objectives. When a careful needs assessment is not conducted, inappropriate programs are more likely to be established. They can be costly (Scharlach et al., 1991).

Secondary Gains

Most companies that surveyed their employee groups were surprised to find that a large proportion of their employees were struggling with dependent care responsibilities (Neal, Chapman, Ingersoll-Dayton, & Emlen, 1993). Awareness of the existence of work and family issues is very valuable to the company and its managers. It can increase their commitment to this issue and to implementing meaningful programs that build goodwill as well as increase productivity. Likewise, unions found survey results most helpful in successfully negotiating work and family programs for their members (*Bargaining for Family Benefits*, 1992).

Special Considerations

To obtain honest answers to the needs assessment, *confidentiality* must be assured. It is easy to do—state on the survey that no names are used at any time, data are gathered in aggregate form, and only the researcher sees the data. Contracting with outside agencies is one way to protect the anonymity of the employee. If in-house staff are used, extra caution needs to be taken to protect employee anonymity.

Finding ways to ensure a *high return rate* on the surveys is another important consideration. Unions have been very successful in using union members to encourage others to complete the survey. They have also used union meetings to encourage full participation (*Bargaining for Family Benefits*, 1992). Companies report the highest return rates when there is visible CEO and upper management support (Neal et.al., 1993). Support is demonstrated when the CEO sends letters pledging support for workplace changes and encouraging employees' support, and when supervisors encourage staff participation. More detailed information on ways to obtain high return rates is presented in Scharlach and colleagues' book, *Elder Care and the Workforce* (1991), and in *Bargaining for Family Benefits* (1992).

Additional Data-Gathering Methods

Although the needs assessment has been shown to be the most precise way to obtain specific information necessary for successful programs, two other methods should be considered: examination of in-house data and convening focus groups.

Obtaining in-house data. Prior to conducting the needs assessment, relevant data can be obtained from in-house files in departments such as personnel, human resources, the employee assistance program (EAP), medical, and compensation and benefits. This data can give clues to the number of employees caring for dependent persons and to problems encountered. For example, personnel files often have information on age, gender, and ethnic characteristics of employees. This information could give some idea of the possible number of persons caring for children or the aged. Employee assistance program utilization information, especially if it includes questions related to caregiving, could give a rough indication of employees with dependent care concerns. Health care utilization data may offer clues to psychosomatic stress ailments, possible indication of worker stress.

Finally, the use of existing benefits can provide important information. For example, a company that does not permit sick days to be used for family emergencies may find a large number of employed women with young children tak-ing an excessive amount of sick time. And high utilization of a dependent care account might indicate the presence of a large number of employees with small children.

Focus groups. After a needs assessment and before moving ahead with expensive work and family programs, focus groups with select employees or union members could be run. Focus groups are often used to determine the likelihood that pro-posed programs would actually be used. This information is necessary before investing a lot of money in a program that upon closer examination would not be utilized much. For example, a focus group might learn that although employees with very frail parents would welcome a respite care program, their parents would not want to use it, perhaps because of strong cultural preferences for family care. Or a focus group might learn that a number of employees with small children would like an on-site center, but they could not afford the proposed cost. For additional information on focus groups see Neal and colleagues' book, *Balancing Work and Caregiving* (1993).

WORK AND FAMILY TASK FORCE

Establishing work and family programs in the workplace is a time-consuming and multi-faceted process. It can take sev-eral years to develop comprehensive programs. One way to approach this process is to establish a task force on work and family issues.

Purpose

Tasks forces generally have two primary purposes. One is to recommend programs that are cost effective to upper man-agement, and/or labor–management committees. The other is to actually implement work and family programs. Some task forces dissolve after the programs have been designed; others form after the design is in place to implement program com-ponents.

Tasks

Tasks performed by the work and family task force will vary according to the task force's purpose. Task forces charged with program design will play an intricate role in the employee needs assessment. They will either approve the approach recommended by an outside vendor, develop an approach themselves, or use some combination of the two. Task forces may also assess the availability and affordability of community resources for dependent care (e.g., child care, respite programs). This information is needed for overall planning. Companies with EAPs may already have such information available for task force use. Some task forces have been responsible for overseeing a pilot program. Pilot projects are a good way to determine, prior to full scale operation, the costs and benefits of a proposed work and family program.

Many factors affect the scope and purpose of the task force: organizational structure, size, level of commitment, and the type of programs that are selected.

Membership

A basic rule of thumb is to have a wide spectrum of persons on the task force without becoming unwieldy. The task force can have both regular members and those who act as consultants to the group. Consultants can include the CEO, an expert in cost benefit analysis, an outside vendor representative, and any one else whose presence would improve the design and coordination of the work and family programs.

Twenty regular employees is the recommended maximum number. There should be a good mix of members by gender, ethnicity, staff–management ratio, type of caregiving responsibility (children, persons with disabilities, frail elders), departmental type, regional interests, and labor–management interests.

Leadership

The primary function of the leadership is to galvanize internal support for the work–family programs and to obtain needed resources to get the job done (Friedman & Johnson, 1991). Leadership most likely will come from human resources, personnel, benefits and compensation, or employee assistance program departments. These departments are often familiar with employees' work and family concerns. Since most of the work and family programs will be incorporated into their departments, staff involvement throughout all phases of development is critical.

Work and family task forces, to be effective, must be well integrated into the work organization. The CEO and upper management's commitment to work and family programs is essential to program success. It is also important to publicize the committee's presence and accomplishments.

Strategic Plans

Staff who develop the strategic plan should consider the following: a) results from the employee needs assessment, b) relevant literature on work and family programs, c) the work organization's readiness for change, d) existing benefits and services, e) community resources and relevant government initiatives related to work and family programs, and f) a proposal for change (*AFL-CIO Working Family Resource Guide*, 1992; *Bargaining For Family Benefits*, 1992; Bureau of National Affairs, 1991a; Lechner, 1992; Scharlach et al., 1991; U.S. Department of Labor, Women's Bureau, 1990; Wagner, Creedon, Sasala, & Neal, 1989).

Needs assessment results. The employee needs assessment will inform the task force of policies, benefits, and services that could help employees better manage their work and family responsibilities. Results from this survey are best used in conjunction with all other considerations.

Work and family literature. Familiarity with the literature on work and family programs will help the task force avoid reinventing the wheel and, thus, increase their efficiency. It also will help the task force develop effective strategies for promoting a work–family agenda.

Readiness for change. Assessing the work organization's interest in work and family programs is a critical step that should not be overlooked by the task force. The Conference Board has developed a one page work sheet that helps assess an organization's level of work–family commitment by evaluating key individuals (e.g., CEO, human resources senior managers, first line supervisor, and many others). This tool can help determine where more promotion of the work–family programs needs to occur (Friedman & Johnson, 1991). Company attitudes such as "if women want careers they shouldn't have children" or "if you give employees an inch they will take a mile" also present barriers to work–family programs (Friedman & Johnson, 1991). Knowing the obstacles is essential for determining effective change strategies.

Existing Benefits and Services. Reviewing existing workplace benefits, policies, and services is an inexpensive and beneficial step for the task force to take. The review may uncover areas that need modification. A common finding among companies that have gone through this review process was underutilization of a workplace program because employees were unaware it existed. By publicizing the program, utilization could be increased. The review process also may uncover that a minor change is needed to make a current work and family program more effective.

Resources for employed caregivers. Efforts should be made by the task force to identify existing community services that working caregivers use or may need. This investigation will determine if there are any service gaps due to access or availability problems. With this information, recommendations for the work organization's involvement can be proposed. For example, if there are not enough child care services for infants and toddlers, and there are a large number of employees who would like this service, community agencies' priorities can be set. This investigation will also help avoid duplication of services. More and more companies and unions are reaching out to their communities. Studies indicate that when such involvement occurs, the community service delivery system is strengthened (Creedon & Tiven, 1989).

The task force also should be cognizant of government initiatives that affect workplace policies and community service development. Informed task force members can play a strong advocacy role in influencing government legislation. Their knowledge of current and forthcoming government legislation is also useful in predicting forthcoming changes and opportunities for public–private partnerships.

Business plan. Finally, knowledge of employee, employer, and community needs and resources, as well as government initiatives, lays the groundwork for the written proposal or business plan. The proposal should include the following: rationale for change; goals and objectives; recommendations for changes at the employee level, supervisory level and community level; time table for implementation; costs and benefits to workplace and/or union; and the evaluation plan.

The business plan should point out how the work–family programs are related to the company's overall business strategies (for example, increased productivity and diversity management). Regarding productivity, the *National Study of the Changing Workforce* reveals that workers with work–family programs "are more likely to stay at their companies and work hard to help their companies succeed" (Galinsky, Bond, & Friedman, 1993, p. 3). Almost 50% of the U.S. work force have dependent care responsibilities. A stable, committed work force improves the quality of services and products of the company. Thus, what is good for employees is good for business.

With increased racial and ethnic diversity in the workplace, companies are realizing that they must "challenge attitudes, practices, and management styles that get in the way of developing each employee's potential" (Friedman & Johnson, 1991, p. 14). Management skills required to deal with diversity issues are the same as those required to deal with work–family issues (Friedman & Johnson, 1991). They require an attitude shift from "one size fits all" to thoughtful, flexible, and creative approaches to maximize each employee's contribution to the workplace.

IMPLEMENTATION

Four issues need to be considered in the implementation phase: Who will manage the new programs? How will they be coordinated? Will partnerships be formed between workplace, union, public, and private groups? How can small businesses develop work and family programs?

Management

Once specific work and family programs are selected, the next step is deciding who will manage these programs. Some companies and most unions rely on staff from their EAPs or MAPs, human resources, welfare funds, and personnel departments to manage the work and family programs. Other companies use a combination of outside vendor with their in-house staff. And a few others seek outside vendors or consultants to manage most aspects of the program. Large companies with extensive work and family programs have created a new position, manager of work and family programs, to oversee the many aspects of their programs (Bureau of National Affairs, 1991b). Recognizing the complexity of program development, one person was deemed necessary to ensure that these new programs were implemented successfully.

Of course, the particular type of work and family program will, to a certain extent, determine administrative authority. For example, a policy on flextime will be established and managed in-house, whereas the management of an on-site child care center will most likely be handled by an external vendor.

In-house programs. When all aspects of work and family programs are managed in-house, they are easier to control and to coordinate. The company or union have direct access to what is happening and they can easily direct the activities. Internal staff are familiar with corporate or union culture and on-going organizational developments that would affect their operations. For example, because they are familiar with common managerial problems, they are in a better position to implement supervisory programs to suit the unique needs of management. Communication with employees is also easier for in-house staff.

A disadvantage of in-house programs is their potential lack of expertise in dealing with employees with family responsibilities. Research on the perceived competency of EAP staff in dealing with employees with elder care concerns indicated that staff did not feel competent addressing these issues (Gorey, Brice, & Rice, 1990). Thus, a well-trained staff is important.

External vendors or consultants. The advantage to going outside the company or union is the likelihood of finding professionals who are experts in specific work and family programs. External providers include specialists in locating resources for children, persons with disabilities, and frail elders; running day care centers; providing elder care case management—to name a few. Most staff are well trained in the emotional as well as the practical concerns of working caregivers. Another advantage of outside programs is that they do not require a long-term commitment; they can be dropped when the contract expires. This gives the company and union more flexibility.

The disadvantage of outside vendors is that they are harder to monitor and some have set packages you must buy whole. Outside vendors also are less familiar with the day-to-day information about the work culture and management issues. Setting up communication channels can be problematic. In some cases, there is limited or no communication between the vendor and the internal EAP. This is a strong disadvantage for the employee, who would benefit from closer communication between the internal and external service.

Regardless of the structure, however, staff involved in providing work and family programs must be well trained in benefits, resource and referral, government initiatives related to working caregivers, communication skills, and case management in cases related to disabled and frail elders. Company or union size, culture, location, and commitment affect decisions on the scope and structure of the work and family programs.

Small Business Consortia

Small businesses and unions may find that implementing work and family programs is too costly. One way they have found to offer these programs is by forming consortia. By pooling their resources, they can implement a variety of programs and keep the costs down. For example, several companies and/or unions might hold a caregivers' fair at a central location. Printing the announcements in bulk reduces the costs and coordinating the task of contacting dozens of providers of elder care services saves time.

One disadvantage to these arrangements is that they are complicated and can easily break down.

MARKETING

Once workplace changes are in place, companies and unions need to aggressively market them. Ongoing communication and education is necessary to insure utilization of services by the maximum number of employees.

Companies and unions recommend that after the initial campaign regarding the introduction of a new benefit, policy, or service, ongoing reminders are necessary. Initial campaigns can include posters, notices in employee and union newsletters, personal letters from the CEO, and upper management, and work site representatives who "talk up" the program directly to their fellow employees. These effective communication methods also can be used in periodic follow-ups.

Sometimes workers, especially those who care for persons with disabilities and frail relatives, do not perceive themselves as caregivers. They consider what they do as an ongoing part of their family experience. This lack of role definition can contribute to underutilization of a workplace program. For this reason, educational materials are needed to help people see themselves more clearly and recognize that they are entitled to certain workplace programs.

SUPERVISOR TRAINING

Training for the supervisors should be an integral part of any work and family program. No matter how carefully work and family program's are planned and implemented, without supervisor support and cooperation, the new program's success can be limited (Wagner et al., 1989). Training sessions have been found to increase supervisors' sensitivity to working caregivers and to increase their helpfulness (Wagner et al., 1989).

Training sessions can focus on work–family program specifics, reasons for their implementation, and ways to effectively communicate to working caregivers supervisors' concerns about utilization of the new programs.

The Families and Work Institute found, through a decade of research on work and family issues, that supervisors are one of the most important parts of successful programs (Galinsky et. al., 1991). They can make or break even well-planned programs.

EVALUATION

Although mentioned last, program evaluation is an integral part of a work and family program. Evaluation components should be linked to program objectives. Well-designed evaluations will enable companies and unions to a) determine how successful the new benefits, services, and policies are; b) identify aspects of the new programs that need to be strengthened; and c) determine if new programs are cost effective. For example, Wagner and Hunt (1992) found in their evaluation of two workplace elder care programs that supervisory support, information about "service resistant" older persons, and information about the full range of benefits (e.g., floating days off, flextime, etc.) could increase program utilization rates.

Evaluation Components

Program evaluations will vary considerably by worksite. However, the most thorough evaluations should assess: a) employee utilization of and satisfaction with work and family programs; b) impact of workplace changes on productivity (absenteeism, performance evaluations), attraction and retention of employees, health care claims, and employee morale; c) competency level of persons, departments, and external vendors administering the new programs; and d) effectiveness of communication and coordination efforts used to promote and administer the new programs.

Some evaluation components are difficult to measure (e.g., work productivity and changes in health care claims) and for this reason are frequently not included. In the long run, however, work organizations should measure these components because they *will* reveal cost effectiveness.

Evaluation Methods

Companies and unions have used a variety of methods to evaluate their programs. Surveys can be designed to determine employee or union member satisfaction and the usefulness of specific work and family programs. Evaluators can conduct focus groups and personal interviews with employees and management to ascertain more detailed information. Management information systems can track utilization rates. Case records, personnel files, health care claims data, and supervisor performance evaluations can all help determine if positive changes in areas such as productivity and health care costs have occurred as a result of the work and family programs.

Although costly and time consuming, the approach used by McDonnell Douglas, which set up a control group of nonusers and followed users and nonusers over a substantial period of time, increased the reliability and generalizability of their findings (Stuart, 1993).

Selection of Evaluators

A rule of thumb in evaluation studies is to have independent evaluators. That is, the person evaluating the program should not be the same person who is responsible for the program. If in-house evaluators are not available, outside consultants with technical skill in program evaluation and familiarity with work and family programs and work organizations would be a good choice. Seeking outside evaluators can be expensive, so colleges and universities may be a cost effective alternative. Some program evaluations have been funded by interested philanthropic foundations.

Program Evaluation Models

Two excellent program evaluations have been reported in the literature. One is the McDonnell Douglas evaluation of its employee assistance program. More information on this study can be obtained by contacting the company in St. Louis, Missouri. The other model program evaluation was funded by the Robert Wood Johnson Foundation to assess the effectiveness of an external vendor's elder care resource and referral services offered to several companies and public agencies. This report, "The Partnership For Eldercare Research Study," can be obtained from the New York City Department for the Aging (Garrison & Jelin, 1990).

REFERENCES

AFL-CIO Department of Employee Benefits. (1992). AFL-CIO Working family resource guide: Putting families first. (1992). Washington, DC: Author.

Bargaining for family benefits: A union member's guide. (1991). New York: Coalition of Labor Union Women.

Bureau of National Affairs. (1991a). *Changing the corporate culture to support work and family programs* (Report No. 42). Washington, DC: Author.

Bureau of National Affairs. (1991b). *The work and family manager: Evolution of a new job* (Report No. 45). Washington, DC: Author.

Creedon, M. A., & Tiven, M. (1989). *Eldercare in the workplace.* Washington, DC: The National Council on the Aging.

Friedman, D. E., & Johnson, A. A. (1991). *Strategies for promoting a work-family agenda.* New York: The Conference Board.

Galinsky, E., Bond, J. T., & Friedman, D. E. (1993). *Highlights: The National Study of the Changing Workforce.* New York: Families and Work Institute.

Galinsky, E., Friedman, D. E., & Hernandez, C. A. (1991). *The cor-*

porate reference guide to work-family programs. New York: Families and Work Institute.

Garrison, A., & Jelin, M. A. (1990). *The partnership for eldercare research study*. New York: New York City Department for the Aging.

Gorey, K. M., Brice, G. C., & Rice, R. W. (1990). An elder care training needs assessment among employee assistance program staff. *Employee Assistance Quarterly*, 5(3), 71–93.

Lechner, V. M. (1992). Family friendly work benefits: Implications for social work managers. In L. M. Healy and B. A. Pine (Eds.), *Managers' choices: Compelling issues in the new decision environment* (pp. 44–56). Florida: National Network for Social Work Managers.

Neal, M. B., Chapman, N. J., Ingersoll-Dayton, B., & Emlen, A. C. (1993). *Balancing work and caregiving for children, adults, and elders*. Newbury Park, CA: Sage.

Scharlach, A. E., Lowe, B. F., & Schneider, E. (1991). *Elder care and the workforce: Blue print for action*. Lexington, MA: Lexington Books.

Stuart, P. (1993). Investments in EAPs pay off. *Personnel Journal*, 72(2), 43–49, 51–52, 54.

U.S. Department of Labor, Women's Bureau, Work and Family Clearinghouse. (1990). *Eldercare program options: Decisionmaking*. Washington, DC: Author.

Wagner, D. L., Creedon, M. A., Sasala, J. M., & Neal, M. B. (1989). *Employees and eldercare: Designing effective responses for the workplace*. CT: The University of Bridgeport.

Wagner, D. L., & Hunt, G. G. (1992). *Factors influencing utilization of workplace programs by employed caregivers*. Poster presented at 45th Annual Meeting of Gerontological Society of America, Washington, DC.

10 Future Directions in Work and Family

This chapter summarizes the major ideas presented in this book. Using this understanding, the authors suggest future agendas for the work and family field.

WHAT WE KNOW TO DATE

Caregiving Experiences

The major findings suggest:

- Employed caregivers have and will continue to care for family members from the youngest to the oldest.
- Employed caregivers of children, persons with disabilities, and frail elderly are expected to increase in numbers.
- Most employed caregivers are women, however, men are showing a small increase in caregiving and household responsibilities.
- Combining work and caregiving is stressful for most caregivers, but not for all.
- Support from family, friends, workplaces, and community agencies buffer some of the stress of managing twin roles.
- Experiences and consequences of managing work and caregiving differ among racial and ethnic groups.

Corporate and Union Responses to Work and Family Concerns

- Responses to employed caregivers have come primarily from large organizations.
- Smaller unions and workplaces give cost factors as primary reasons for nonparticipation.
- Most frequently implemented benefits, services, and policies include lower cost items such as granting flextime, allowing use of sick days for family illness, and providing child and elder care resource and referral services.
- The most committed work organizations add supervisory training, community investments, and mission statements that legitimize employees' family concerns.
- Although a natural player in the work and family arena, EAPs and MAPs have been slow to lead.
- Unions have also been reticent to lead in work and family concerns, although some unions have been very successful in negotiating for work and family benefits.
- Some industries (e.g., health care and telecommunications) have been much more responsive to dependent care than others.

Community Responses to Work and Family Needs

Major findings suggest:

- There is a great need for more extensive child care (including children with disabilities), dependent adult care, and elder care services in many communities.
- Profit and not-for-profit vendors specializing in child and elder care services have proliferated in the past five to ten years. Most of these services are unlicensed and unregulated, leading to quality of care concerns.
- Workplaces increasingly are contracting with resource and referral vendors to provide this service to their employees. They also are beginning to rely on external vendors for EAPs and managed care services.
- Community services for children, persons with disabili-

ties, and frail elders are not evenly dispersed throughout the United States.

- Employed caregivers most in need of affordable community services for dependent family members have difficulty obtaining and paying for these services.
- Local service providers need training in pricing and marketing their services. They need to organize and hire bargaining agents for negotiations with national vendors.

Government Responses

- Historically, the United States' preference for limited government intervention in family and work domains has retarded leadership in area of work and family concerns.
- Recent passage of the Family and Medical Leave Act suggests that the Clinton administration may be more active.
- Federal, state, and local government employees also need dependent care assistance and some jurisdictions have been more responsive than others.
- Government policies, particularly tax policies, can provide significant incentives to employers to develop work–family programs and can encourage employees to use such services.
- Public–private partnerships will continue to grow in the 1990s as budget constraints force companies, unions, and service agencies and government to share resources.

FUTURE DIRECTIONS IN WORK
AND FAMILY DOMAINS

Three areas deserve special attention as we look into the 21st century: knowledge, leadership, and equity.

Knowledge

Although many research studies have been done in the work and family area, few studies have focused on nonwhite, non–middle class caregivers. We know far more about the middle class, married, employed caregiver than we know about employed single mothers; gay and lesbian caregivers; African-American, Asian, and nonwhite Hispanic caregivers; and employees caring for persons with disabilities. The United States is becoming far more diverse in its population makeup and family structure. Longitudinal studies using samples from diverse groups are needed to identify similarities and differences between the majority group's experiences and those of minorities, gays and lesbians, and employees caring for persons with disabilities. Researchers and funding sources must make diversity a prime consideration in project goals.

We also need more studies on the effectiveness of workplace interventions targeted to working caregivers. Demonstration projects which have been few in number, can help employers identify the most valuable and cost effective programs. Research institutions can be approached to help unions and companies with limited funds conduct program evaluation studies.

A national conference of researchers and practitioners could be held to share information, crystallize ideas, and develop clearer research agendas. A few years ago, the National Institute on Aging, in cooperation with the New York Business Group on Health, held a conference for researchers, practitioners, and employers on general issues related to elder care. It is time for another conference to focus on employed caregivers from diverse groups and program effectiveness.

Leadership and Cooperation

Large work organizations, not the government, have assumed the leadership role in the development of programs that offer support to employed caregivers. Such developments are beneficial to only a small number of employed caregivers. Additionally, it is not the nature of the business community to be concerned with the quality and affordability of the range of community services established for children, persons with disabilities, and frail elders. Furthermore, when companies reach out to community vendors to provide services to their employees, employees at other companies may be disadvantaged. There may be no child care openings for them because the larger company has taken those slots.

Leadership in the 21st century needs to focus on all employed caregivers at all work situations. This type of leadership can not come from the business community alone. It must include government at the local, state, and federal levels, and the vendors that offer services to employed caregivers. Partnerships between these major players need to be formed.

Historically, the United States has been reluctant for government to take an active role in the affairs of workplaces, families, and service providers. The capitalist viewpoint has been that consumer services (in this case those for employed caregivers) will be available at the best price if providers are free to negotiate prices with the consumer, uninhibited by government regulations. Government interventions, according to this theory, can lead to unnecessary red tape and high costs for new product development.

Workplaces, when involved in government decision making, generally take a defensive position, trying to ward off costly regulations and increased welfare benefits. These tensions make it difficult for workplaces and service providers to come together with government officials to develop a "Marshall Plan" for all employed caregivers.

Work organizations have taken some small steps in collaborating with others, as described earlier. They bring to planning and decision making meetings a rich experience in the development of family-focused benefits and services. They can, however, go further to help shape the child and elder care services of tomorrow.

Equity Issues

In the United States family-focused benefits, services, and policies are not uniformly provided to all employed caregivers. Employed caregivers most in need of assistance are least likely to receive these services. Single mothers are concentrated in low-paying service jobs with few benefits. Gay and lesbian employed caregivers are often excluded from availing themselves of workplace programs either due to fear of "coming out" or actual exclusionary clauses. Male caregivers still experience cultural taboos against utilizing family benefits. Minorities are overrepresented in the low-paying jobs least likely to offer family-focused benefits, services, and policies.

A few notable broad human service proposals are in their early stages of development. If they come to fruition, these universal and comprehensive plans would have an impact on all employed caregivers. One is the early childhood education movement, the other is the universal health care plan.

Child care and education. Child care services in this country are inadequate for most employed parents, but particularly for low-income and nonwhite parents, as established in Chapters 2 and 3. One solution to this problem is to revamp the entire child care system. There is a movement under foot that calls for using the public schools as the base for providing high-quality, affordable, and developmentally appropriate child care services.

The "School of the 21st Century" as proposed by child expert and advocate, Edward Zigler (1991) would be open all day and year-round to accommodate preschoolers and school-aged children during their nonschool hours. Fees would be charged on a sliding scale. Child care workers would be well trained and paid a decent income. Activities for the children would be age appropriate and developmentally challenging. Staff would be familiar with community social and health care services and assist parents in obtaining them. Parental involvement would be expected. Quality controls that are appropriately flexible would be in place.

The purpose of the School of the 21st Century and similar models is to provide all children with high-quality, affordable child care. Advocates of this comprehensive education and care system believe it simultaneously addresses "our nation's urgent education, economic development, and work force priorities, as well as the development needs of children" (Topol, 1993, p. 1).

As testimony to this movement, significant national conferences have been held to inform and move to action leaders in business, child care, local communities, education, government, and research. In 1993, two important conferences were held: the Child Care Action Campaign and the Council of Chief State School Officers cosponsored "Child Care and Education: The Critical Connection," and the Families and Work Institute and the National Association for the Education of Young Children cosponsored the "National Forum on State and Community Planning in Early Education and Care." Most advocates believe the present Clinton administration is open to making a systemic change in how children receive care while their parents work.

Health care for all. The Clinton administration is working on a health care plan that would include all Americans. The planners are considerating coverage for long-term health care needs for the older generation and for chronic medical conditions in the younger generation. A repeated problem of employed caregivers to the elderly is obtaining those services that are needed to maintain the frail elder in the home. These services include: home health care, companionship, adult day care, and transportation assistance, to name a few. If the universal health plan is passed, it will alleviate much of the burden on the employed caregiver who often is trying to manage work and caregiving at the same time. It is hoped that this plan will simplify access to and improve coordination of long-term care services.

We believe the United States is moving ahead on providing child care and health care to all because it is in the best interest of our country to support families. The children of today are the workers of tomorrow. They need nurturance to prepare them for productive lives. Our senior citizens and their employed relatives need adequate assistance.

Gender roles. A third issue concerning equity is the division of male and female responsibilities for the care of dependent persons and for the home. Women hold a far greater share of this domain, even though they work almost as many hours as their male counterparts. Workplace and government legislation encouraging male participation in caregiving tasks will help equalize role sharing. The greatest change that needs to come, however, is in men's and women's attitudes about dependent care responsibility. We believe that more dialogue is needed between male and female caregivers to find ways to share more equally these very important responsibilities.

Costs for New Programs

The United States does not have unlimited resources. Comprehensive and universal health and child care services are expensive. While all may recognize the need, few address the costs. Perhaps it is true that a penny spent now will save dollars later, but the reality is that initial costs for these new programs will be considerable. For this reason, progress will be slow and many compromises will be made.

We believe hard decisions will have to be made in the following areas: health care services, income distribution, and use of property taxes to pay for education. Can this country continue to pay for unlimited health services? One way to contain health costs is to limit, to a far greater degree than present, reimbursement for medical procedures for persons with limited benefit from these services. Oregon is experimenting with such an approach and Canada has had cutoff points for some time. It is very hard to make these life and death decisions. Our country, with the great value we place on individual freedom, will find this struggle very painful. But we must face these decisions if we want to provide long-term care services and basic health care coverage for all citizens.

The second area concerns income distribution. Should the well-to-do be expected to pay higher taxes to help pay for comprehensive health and child care services? Will senior citizens in the higher tax brackets be taxed a greater amount for their social security and medicare benefits? Opponents to increasing taxes on the rich say the wealthy need their money to reinvest and create jobs. Yet, can we expect children to go without? Hard decisions concerning equity issues must be made.

The final decision-making area is financing for education and child care services. Presently, local communities, through their property taxes, pay for the schools in their area. This arrangement leads to the creation of rich and poor schools. Communities with low-cost housing bring in fewer property tax dollars. One approach to equalizing school financing is to put property tax money into larger pools and to spread it around. America's value of rugged individualism makes this approach seem very unfair to persons in wealthier communities. Yet, all children need appropriate care and should be entitled to a similar education. These battles will be fought when cost considerations enter the discussion.

CONCLUSION

We have seen rapid change in workplace responses to care-givers in the past 20 years. Today, minimum leave policies are mandated by law; tax incentives encourage dependent care assistance plans; unions explicitly bargain for work–family benefits; major corporations boast about their work–family benefits. We even have intergenerational day care at some corporate locations. So there has been progress.

In the next decade and thereafter we will experience a rapid growth in the number of elderly dependents, and almost certainly we will experience similar growth in the number of dependent adults. The greatest children population increases will be in the Hispanic and Asian Pacific communities. The working caregiver population will face changing demands. The workplace will need to adapt to these demographic changes and develop new responses to a more diverse work force.

We hope to see a more cohesive public–private partnership emerge on the national level so that I&R, for example, can be comprehensive and available to all without duplication of service. The baby boom generation is maturing; they will determine in large measure the quality of government, public, and voluntary care services in the year 2000.

REFERENCES

Topol, D. (1993). Child care and education: The critical connection. *Childcare ActioNews, 10*, 1, 3.

Zigler, E. F., & Lang, M. E. (1991). *Child care choices*. New York: The Free Press.

Appendix A

RESOURCE ORGANIZATIONS

Aging Network Services
4400 East-West Highway, Suite 907
Bethesda, MD 20814
301-986-1608

Alliance of Businesses for Childcare Development
600 Wiltshire Blvd., Suite 440
Los Angeles, CA 90017
213-624-7018

American Association of Retired Persons
601 E St. NW
Washington, DC 20049
202-434-2245

American Society on Aging
833 Market St., Suite 512
San Francisco, CA 94103
703-543-2617

Association of Child Care Consultants, Inc.
1801 Peachtree St. NE, Suite 160
Atlanta, GA 30309
404-352-8137

Association of Child Care Consultants, Inc.
Cornerstone
450 Bedford St.
Lexington, MA 02173
617-862-8000

Bank Street College of Education
Center for Children's Policy
610 West 112th St.
New York, NY 10025
212-875-4759

Bay Area Dependent Care Coalition
c/o Women's Bureau, US Dept. of Labor
71 Stevenson St., Suite 927
San Francisco, CA 94105
415-744-6679

Boston University Center on Work and Family
One University Road
Boston, MA 02215
617-353-7225

Buck Consultants
176 Federal St.
Boston, MA 02110
617-951-0535

Bureau of National Affairs
1231 25th St. NW
Washington, DC 20037
202-452-4501

Burud and Associates
56 East Holly, Suite 215
Pasadena, CA 91103
818-796-8258

Center for Corporate Health,Inc
10467 White Granite Drive
Oakton, VA 22124
800-745-1333

Chicago Metropolitan Work and Family Council
200 South Michigan Ave., Suite 1520
Chicago, IL 60604
312-341-0900

Child Care Resource and Research Unit
Center for Urban and Community Studies
University of Toronto
455 Spadina Ave.
Toronto, ONT M5S2G8
416-978-6895

Conference Board
Work and Family Information Center
845 Third Ave.
New York, NY 10022
212-759-0900

Conference Board of Canada
225 Smythe Rd.
Ottawa, CA K1H8M7
613-526-3280

Coopers & Lybrand
217 East Redwood St.
Baltimore, MD 21202
410-783-7629

Corporate Health Consultants
1505 Hurontario St.
Mississauga, ONT L5G3H7
416-278-1501

The Creedon Group
8214 Bucknell Dr.
Vienna, VA 22180
703-849-9565

Dependent Care Connection
PO Box 2783
Westport, CT 06880
203-332-0102

Families and Work Institute
330 Seventh Ave.
New York, NY 10001
212-465-2044

Family Service America
11700 West Lake Park Dr.
Park Place
Milwaukee, WI 53224
414-359-1040

Health Action Forum of Greater Boston
c/o Frank B. Hall & Co.
89 Broad St.
Boston, MA 02110
617-482-3100 x 321

Initiatives
PO Box 68
Doylestown, PA 18901
215-348-1432

Metropolitan Washington Council of Governments
Work & Family Coalition
777 North Capitol St. SE
Washington, DC 20002-4226
202-962-3200

National Association of Area Agencies on Aging
1112 16th St. NW
Washington, DC 20036
202-296-8134

National Council on the Aging
4th St. SW
Washington, DC
202-479-1200

National Association of Child Care Resource
and Referral Agencies
PO Box 40246
Washington, DC 20016
202-333-4194

National Association of Employee Benefits Administrators
c/o Barcelona & Co.
12416 South Harlem Ave.
Palos Heights, IL 60643
708-448-8077

National Association of Private Geriatric Care Managers
655 North Alverton Way, Suite 108
Tucson, AZ 85711
602-881-8008

National Council of Jewish Women
53 West 23rd St., 6th Floor
New York, NY 10010
212-645-4048

New York Business Group on Health
622 Third Ave.
New York, NY 10017-6763

Ontario Women's Directorate
Consultative Services Branch
Suite 200, 480 University Ave.
Toronto, ONT M5G1V2
416-597-4570

Partnership for Eldercare
(New York City Dept on Aging)
280 Broadway
New York, NY 10007
212-442-3113

Partnership Group
840 West Main St.
Lansdale, PA 19446
215-362-5918

Portland State University
Regional Research Institute for Human Services
PO Box 751
Portland, OR 97207-0751
503-725-3000

Society for Human Resource Management
606 North Washington St.
Alexandria, VA 22314
703-548-3440

Vanier Institute of the Family
120 Holland Ave.
Ottawa, Ontario K1Y0X6
613-722-4007

Women's Bureau Work and Family Clearinghouse
U.S. Department of Labor
200 Constitution Ave. NW
Washington, DC 20210
202-523-6611

Work/Family Directions
930 Commonwealth Ave.
Boston, MA 02215
617-278-4000

Appendix B

EMPLOYEE SURVEY

INSTRUCTIONS: Thank you for participating in our survey. Please enter your answer (number or letter) to the right of each question in the box provided. Also please note that every employee completes the first two pages of questions; however, the remaining questions are completed only if applicable. Consequently, the questionnaire is not as time consuming as it may appear. All responses are anonymous; you will not be identified in any way. We appreciate your frank answers.

1. Your age and sex? ("M"=male; "F"=female)

    years   sex

2. Your occupation?
   1. Professional or technical specialist (non-nursing)
   2. Managerial or administrative
   3. Registered nurse
   4. L.P.N./Aide
   5. Sales
   6. Clerical
   7. Skilled crafts (carpenter, mechanic, electrician, etc.)
   8. Mail carrier
   9. Service (food, housekeeping, laundry, maintenance, security, aide)
   10. Sawmill worker
   11. Logger/cutter
   12. Machine or heavy-equipment operator
   13. Transport operator (truck or bus driver)
   14. Warehouse worker
   15. Non-farm labor
   16. Other: _____

173

3. Your job status?
   1. Full-time
   2. Part-time
   3. On call/relief

[16]

4. Your job shift?
   1. Days   4. Rotating
   2. Swing/evenings 5. Weekend only
   3. Nights   6. Other

[17]

5. Usual number of days worked per week?

[18]
days

6. Average number of hours worked per week?

[19   20]
hours

7. Do you work Saturdays or Sundays as part of your scheduled work?   1. Yes   2. No

[21]

8. The amount of time it usually takes you to travel one way from home to work?

[22   23]
minutes

9. The zip code of your home address?

[24   28]
zip code

10. How long have you worked for this employer?

[29]   [32]
years   months

11. In the past four weeks:

   How many days have you missed work other than vacation?

[33   34]
days

   How many times have you been late to work?

[35   36]
times

   How many times have you left work early or left during the day?

[37   38]
times

   While at work, how many times have you been interrupted (including telephone calls) to deal with family-related matters?

[39   40]
times

12. Other than vacation, how many days have you missed work in the past **three months**?

[41   42]
times

174

13. How much flexibility do you have in your work schedule to handle family responsibilities?
    1. A lot of flexibility
    2. Some flexibility
    3. Hardly any flexibility
    4. No flexibility at all

    [43]

14. Do you have a spouse (or partner)   1. Yes   [44]
    who lives in your household?   2. No

15. If you have a spouse (or partner) in your household, does he or she work outside the home?
    0. Not applicable
    1. Yes, full-time
    2. Yes, part-time
    3. No

    [45]

16. If you have an employed spouse (or partner) in your household, does he or she work the same shift as you?
    0. Not applicable
    1. Same Shift
    2. Partly overlapping shifts
    3. Different, non-overlapping shifts

    [46]

17. If you have an employed spouse (or partner) in your household, will he or she also be completing this survey?
    0. Not applicable
    1. Yes, works for the same employer
    2. Yes, works somewhere else
    3. No
    4. Don't know

    [47]

18. What is the approximate annual gross income of your household?
    1. Under $10,000
    2. $10,000-$14,999
    3. $15,000-$19,999
    4. $20,000-$24,999
    5. $25,000-$29,999
    6. $30,000-$39,999
    7. $40,000-$49,999
    8. $50,000-$59,999
    9. $60,000-$69,999
    10. $70,000 or more

    [48 | 49]

19. What is your own <u>personal</u> annual gross income?
    1. Under $10,000
    2. $10,000-$14,999
    3. $15,000-$19,999
    4. $20,000-$24,999
    5. $25,000-$29,999
    6. $30,000-$39,999
    7. $40,000-$49,999
    8. $50,000-$59,999
    9. $60,000-$69,999
    10. $70,000 or more

50	51

20. <u>Other than yourself and your spouse</u>, are you eligible to claim any of the following persons as a dependent or exemption on your federal or state income tax?

Children?
    1. Yes
    2. No
    3. Don't know

52

Person(s) 65 or older?
    1. Yes
    2. No
    3. Don't know

53

Disabled Adults?
    1. Yes
    2. No
    3. Don't know

54

21. Do you believe that family responsibilities have held back your career?
    1. Definitely
    2. Somewhat
    3. A little
    4. Not at all

55

22. Circumstances differ and some people find it easier than others to combine working with family responsibilities. In general, how easy or difficult is it for you?
    1. Very easy
    2. Easy
    3. Somewhat easy
    4. Somewhat difficult
    5. Difficult
    6. Very difficult

56

176

23. We would like to know which areas of life are creating difficulty, worry, or stress for people. In the past 4 weeks, to what extent have any of the following areas of life been a source of stress to you?

Your health:
1. No stress at all
2. Hardly any stress
3. Some stress
4. A lot of stress

| 57 |

Health of other family members:
1. No stress at all
2. Hardly any stress
3. Some stress
4. A lot of stress

| 58 |

Child care:
0. Not applicable
1. No stress at all
2. Hardly any stress
3. Some stress
4. A lot of stress

| 59 |

Care for elderly or disabled adult family members:
0. Not applicable
1. No stress at all
2. Hardly any stress
3. Some stress
4. A lot of stress

| 60 |

Personal or family finances:
1. No stress at all
2. Hardly any stress
3. Some stress
4. A lot of stress

| 61 |

Your job:
1. No stress at all
2. Hardly any stress
3. Some stress
4. A lot of stress

| 62 |

Family relationships, including extended family:
1. No stress at all
2. Hardly any stress
3. Some stress
4. A lot of stress

| 63 |

24. Do you have children under 18 (including your spouse's children) living in your household?

1. Yes
2. No

| 64 |

If you have no children under 18 living in your household, please go to question #49 on page 5. If you do have children under 18 living in your household, please complete the following questions about the arrangements that you make for your children while you are at work. By "arrangements" we mean any way that children spend time or are supervised, including being home with your spouse, looking after themselves, or going to a child care program.

177

25. What are the ages (years) and sex (M=male, F=female) of the children under 18 living in your household? List the youngest to oldest. For children under 1 year, put "B" for baby.

26. Now we would like to get a picture of the child care arrangements (other than regular school) that you use while you are at work. Listed below are various child care arrangements; next to them are boxes for each child listed in question #26. For each child, please write the usual number of hours per week that each arrangement is used while you are at work or going to or from work; if not used, leave blank. For example, if your child spends 30 hours a week in a child care center and 10 more with your spouse at home, write a "30" and "10" in those boxes for that child.

At home with my spouse/partner

At home with an adult relative (18 or over)

At home with an adult non-relative (18 or over)

At home with a non-relative under 18 (sitter)

At home with an older brother or sister under 18

At home, looking after self

In the home of a relative or ex-spouse

In the home of a non-relative ("family daycare")

In a child care center or nursery school (not public kindergarten)

In after-school activities such as sports, clubs, or job

27. How satisfied are you with the child care arrangement or combination of arrangements for each child? Using the scale below, write the number of your response in the column for each child.
1. Very satisfied
2. Satisfied
3. Mixed Feelings
4. Dissatisfied
5. Very dissatisfied

28. Do any of your children have a physical, emotional, or developmental disability? If so, please circle his/her age at the top of the column.

178

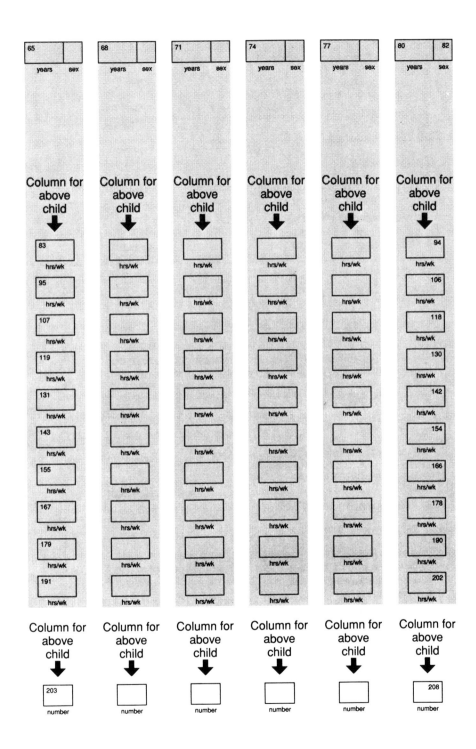

65		68		71		74		77		80		82
years	sex	years	sex	years	sex	years	sex	years	sex	years		sex

Column for above child ↓ | Column for above child ↓ | Column for above child ↓ | Column for above child ↓ | Column for above child ↓ | Column for above child ↓

83 hrs/wk	hrs/wk	hrs/wk	hrs/wk	hrs/wk	94 hrs/wk
95 hrs/wk	hrs/wk	hrs/wk	hrs/wk	hrs/wk	106 hrs/wk
107 hrs/wk	hrs/wk	hrs/wk	hrs/wk	hrs/wk	118 hrs/wk
119 hrs/wk	hrs/wk	hrs/wk	hrs/wk	hrs/wk	130 hrs/wk
131 hrs/wk	hrs/wk	hrs/wk	hrs/wk	hrs/wk	142 hrs/wk
143 hrs/wk	hrs/wk	hrs/wk	hrs/wk	hrs/wk	154 hrs/wk
155 hrs/wk	hrs/wk	hrs/wk	hrs/wk	hrs/wk	166 hrs/wk
167 hrs/wk	hrs/wk	hrs/wk	hrs/wk	hrs/wk	178 hrs/wk
179 hrs/wk	hrs/wk	hrs/wk	hrs/wk	hrs/wk	190 hrs/wk
191 hrs/wk	hrs/wk	hrs/wk	hrs/wk	hrs/wk	202 hrs/wk

Column for above child ↓ | Column for above child ↓ | Column for above child ↓ | Column for above child ↓ | Column for above child ↓ | Column for above child ↓

| 203 number | number | number | number | number | 208 number |

179

29. If you use child care in a non-relative's home ("family day care"):

How far is it from your home?

215

0. Not applicable
1. Next door
2. 1 or 2 blocks
3. ¼ mile
4. ½ mile
5. 1 mile
6. 2 miles
7. 4 miles
8. 8 miles
9. over 8 miles

Using the same choices above, how far is it from your work?

216

30. If you use a child care center or nursery school (but not public kindergarten):

How far is it from your home?

217

0. Not applicable
1. Next door
2. 1 or 2 blocks
3. ¼ mile
4. ½ mile
5. 1 mile
6. 2 miles
7. 4 miles
8. 8 miles
9. over 8 miles

Using the same choices above, how far is it from your work?

218

31. What things do you dislike (if any) about your current child care arrangements? Check all that apply.

1. I don't dislike anything

219

2. Too far from home

220

3. Cost too high

221

4. Don't like program

222

5. Don't like caregiver

223

6. Too many kids

224

7. Worried about safety

225

8. Too dirty or unsanitary

226

9. Other: _____

227

32. If your child looks after him/herself or is cared for by an older brother or sister while you are at work, what makes it possible for you to use this arrangement? (Check all that apply.)

1. My child is mature enough

   ☐ 228

2. I can't find any better alternatives

   ☐ 229

3. My child doesn't want to do anything else

   ☐ 230

4. I have an older child whom I feel confident in

   ☐ 231

5. I'm accessible at work

   ☐ 232

6. My child wants more independence

   ☐ 233

7. I have good neighbors

   ☐ 234

8. I can't afford anything else

   ☐ 235

9. Transportation to anything else is a problem

   ☐ 236

33. How often have you changed child care arrangements in the past year?

   ☐ 237 238
   times

34. Do you plan to change your child care arrangements in the near future?   1. Yes   2. No

   ☐ 239

35. When a child is sick, employed parents often have to choose between going to work and staying home. When one of your children is sick and you stay home, which of the following is most likely to make it possible? (Check all that apply.)

1. I use sick leave.

   ☐ 240

2. I have flexible hours.

   ☐ 241

3. I take a day off without pay.

   ☐ 242

4. I use vacation.

   ☐ 243

5. I do my work at home.

   ☐ 244

6. Other: _____

   ☐ 245

181

36. About how much extra time (minutes) does your travel for child care add to your daily round trip travel time to and from work? If none, put "0".

246	247

minutes

37. To what extent do the management practices in your department, branch or office make it easy or difficult for you to deal with child care problems during working hours?
   1. Very easy
   2. Easy
   3. Somewhat easy
   4. Somewhat difficult
   5. Difficult
   6. Very difficult

248

38. In your experience, how easy or difficult has it been to find child care arrangements?
   1. Very easy
   2. Easy
   3. Somewhat easy
   4. Somewhat difficult
   5. Difficult
   6. Very difficult

249

39. How easy or difficult has it been to continue or maintain child care arrangements?
   1. Very easy
   2. Easy
   3. Somewhat easy
   4. Somewhat difficult
   5. Difficult
   6. Very difficult

250

40. How much does child care cost you per month (if any)? For each type of child care that you use, write the average dollars per month that it costs.

In non-relative's home ("family day care")

251	254

dollars/mo.

In a relative's home

255	258

dollars/mo.

Someone who provides care in my home

259	262

dollars/mo.

Child care center or nursery school

263	266

dollars/mo.

Other: _____

267	270

41. How easy or difficult has it been to pay for child care arrangements?
    0. I don't pay for child care
    1. Very easy
    2. Easy
    3. Somewhat easy
    4. Somewhat difficult
    5. Difficult
    6. Very difficult

    [271]

42. Through your employer, do you use a plan that allows you to be reimbursed for your child care expenses with before-tax dollars?   1. Yes   2. No

    [272]

43. Do you claim a tax credit for child care? In other words, on your federal income tax return, do you claim any expenses that you pay for child care?   1. Yes   2. No

    [273]

44. In your family, who takes responsibility for child care arrangements?
    1. I do completely.
    2. Mostly I do.
    3. Equally shared with spouse or other.
    4. Mostly spouse or other does.
    5. Spouse or other does completely.

    [274]

45. Do child care considerations limit the number of hours you work?
    1. Yes, that's why I work part-time.
    2. Yes, that's why my spouse works part-time.
    3. Yes, that's why my spouse is not employed.
    4. Only a little.
    5. Not at all.

    [275]

46. Would you work a different shift, if you could get it?
    1. Yes, if I could find child care to go with it.
    2. Yes, and child care is not an issue.
    3. No

    [276]

47. Would you work more hours, if you had the shift and child care you wanted?
    1. Yes, if I had the child care.
    2. Yes, if only I had the shift I wanted.
    3. No, I'm working just about as many hours as I want to.
    4. No, I'm already working more hours than I want to.

    [277]

48. In the past year, have you called or gone to an agency for any of the following services relating to child care. (Check all that apply.)

1. Yes, for referral or help in finding resources. `278`

2. Yes, for counseling or advice. `279`

3. Yes, for a child care service for a sick child. `280`

4. No, but I would have found it useful. `281`

5. No, I didn't know of any such services. `282`

6. No, I got all the help I needed from others (friends, neighbors, relatives, church, school, etc.) `283`

49. Employees may have responsibilities for helping out adult relatives or friends who are elderly or disabled. By "disabled" we mean physically handicapped, frail, chronically ill, developmentally handicapped or seriously emotionally handicapped. By "helping out" we mean help with shopping, home maintenance or transportation, checking on by phone, providing care, making arrangements for care, etc. This includes persons who live with the employee or who live somewhere else. Which of the following best describes your situation? (Choose one.)

1. I currently have responsibilities for helping an elderly or disabled adult.

2. I don't have responsibilities for helping an elderly or disabled adult but probably will in the future.

3. I don't have responsibilities for helping an elderly or disabled adult but possibly will in the future.

4. I don't have responsibilities for helping an elderly or disabled adult and probably won't in the future. `284`

If you answered "1" to the above question, that is, if you currently provide help to an elderly or disabled adult, please answer the questions below; if not, please go to the bottom of page 6 and give us your comments.

50. How many elderly or disabled persons are you currently helping? `285`
number

51. For each person, tell us his or her age.

`286` years `years` `years` `293` years

52. Do any of these persons live in your household?   1. Yes   2. No `294`

184

53. Do any of these persons live 100 or more miles away from you?

1. Yes
2. No

`295`

54. On average, how many hours per week do you help this person(s)?

`296` `297`

hours

55. In the past year, when this person(s) has needed help, who has usually been the one who has given it or seen that it was given?
   1. I have been the only one.
   2. I have been the main one with some help.
   3. I have shared equally with other(s).
   4. Other(s), with my help.

`298`

56. What do you personally contribute to the cost of caring for this person or persons per month?

`299` `302`

dollars/mo.

57. Through your employer, do you use a plan that allows you to be reimbursed for your adult dependent care expenses with before-tax dollars?

1. Yes
2. No

`303`

58. Do you claim an income tax credit for any adult dependent care expenses? In other words, on your federal tax return, do you claim any expenses that you pay for such care as nursing services or adult day care?

1. Yes
2. No

`304`

59. While you are at work, who provides care for or helps this person(s)? Check as many arrangements as applicable. Also, rate your satisfaction with these arrangements using the scale below.
   1. Very satisfied
   2. Satisfied
   3. Mixed feelings
   4. Dissatisfied
   5. Very dissatisfied

	Arrangements (check)	Satisfaction (number)
Looks after self	`305`	`306`
Adult relative or family member	`307`	`308`
Someone who was hired	`309`	`310`
Volunteer or unpaid visitor	`311`	`312`
Adult day care	`313`	`314`
Nursing home or care facility	`315`	`316`
Other: _____	`317`	`318`

185

60. When the person you are caring for needs assistance and you take time off from work, which of the following is most likely to make it possible? (Check all that apply.)
   1. I use sick leave.

   2. I have flexible hours.

   3. I take a day off without pay.

   4. I use vacation.

   5. I do my work at home.

   6. Other: _____

319	
320	
321	
322	
323	
324	

61. To what extent do the management practices in your department, branch or office make it easy or difficult for you to deal with adult dependent care problems during working hours?
   1. Very easy
   2. Easy
   3. Somewhat easy
   4. Somewhat difficult
   5. Difficult
   6. Very difficult

325	

62. In your experience, how easy or difficult has it been to find care arrangements for this elderly or disabled person(s)?
   0. Not applicable
   1. Very easy
   2. Easy
   3. Somewhat easy
   4. Somewhat difficult
   5. Difficult
   6. Very difficult

326	

63. How easy or difficult has it been for you to provide care or help to this elderly or disabled person(s)?
   1. Very easy
   2. Easy
   3. Somewhat easy
   4. Somewhat difficult
   5. Difficult
   6. Very difficult

327	

64. People who have responsibilities for providing adult care often have difficulty knowing where to turn for help. How easy or difficult has it been for you?
   1. Very easy
   2. Easy
   3. Somewhat easy
   4. Somewhat difficult
   5. Difficult
   6. Very difficult

328	

186

65. In the past year, have you called or gone to an agency for any of the following services relating to the care of, or help for, adult family members or friends? (Check all that apply.)

1. Yes, for referral or help in finding resources. 329

2. Yes, for counseling or advice. 330

3. Yes, for a respite-care service. 331

4. No, but I would have found it useful. 332

5. No, I didn't know of any such services. 333

6. No, I got all the help I needed from others (friends, neighbors, relatives, church, school, etc.) 334

Please give us your comments. 335

Thank you for answering the survey questions. Please return this questionnaire in the envelope provided.

Index

Comprehensive Alcohol Abuse
and Alcoholism Prevention,
90
Corporate model, employee
assistance program, 85–
86
Corporate response to work-family
issues, 55–58
extent of workplace benefits,
57–58
stages of workplace response,
57

D

Demographic changes
disabled children, dependents,
7–8
elderly persons at home,
employees with, 4–7
elderly population, 4–7
ethnic caregivers, 39–43
ethnic employment rate, 1–2
family income, 3
female employment rate, 1–2
gay and lesbian caregivers, 43
household services, 2–3
long-distance caregivers, 45–
48
male caregiving, 32–36
productivity of work
organizations, 8–9
single mothers, 36–39
working parent, 3–4
Dependent care assistance plans,
59, 72–73
usage rate, 72
Disabled dependents, employees
with, demographic changes,
7–8
Downsize, of work-family program,
9
Drug-Free Workplace Act of 1988,
90
Dual-earner families, 3. *See also*
Two-parent families

E

Economic Recovery Tax Act of
1981, 59
Eldercare program
employee assistance program,
86
forces shaping, 86–91
government legislation, 90
ideology, 87
managed care, 88
organizational climate, 88–89
serving troubled employee,
87–88
technology, 91
union-based *vs.* corporate-
based, 89
Elderly persons at home,
employees with,
demographic changes, 4–7
Employed fathers, 4, 13, 14
Employed mothers, 13
Employed parents, 3
child care, 15
Employee absence, 24
Employee assistance program
background information, 82–83
corporate model, 85–86
eldercare program, 86
models of, 84
promise of, in work and family
area, 95–96
union model, 84–85
ways to strengthen
advocacy, 93
employee needs assessment,
91–92
expansion and coordination of
services, 92–93
external vendors, 94
in-service training, 92
national leadership, 94–95
program evaluation, 93–94
state leadership, 94–95
work and family assistance
program, 84–85

Springer Publishing Company

GENDER ISSUES ACROSS THE LIFE CYCLE

Barbara Rubin Wainrib, EdD, Editor

This diverse and fascinating volume goes beyond simply helping to sharpen the existing models of male and female adult development. It probes the implications of those developmental and social shifts for clinicians struggling with day-to-day gender issues arising within the clinical context. The result is a richly conceived and well-executed exploration of issues that are basic to us all—as people and as practitioners.

Partial Contents:

Who's Who and What's What: The Effects of Gender on Development in Adolescence, *W. J. Cosse* • Clinical Issues in the Treatment of Adolescent Girls, *A. Rubenstein* • The Worst of Both Worlds: Dilemmas of Contemporary Young Women, *N. McWilliams* • Gender Issues of the Young Adult Male, *M. Goodman* • The New Father Roles, *R. F. Levant* • The Thirty-Something Woman: To Career or Not to Career, *F. L. Denmark* • Thirty-Plus and Not Married, *F.W. Kaslow* • Motherhood in the Age of Reproductive Technology, *S. G. Mikesel* • Motherhood and Women's Gender Role Journeys: A Metaphor for Healing, Transition, and Transformation, *J. M. O'Neil and J. Eagan* • Helping Men at Midlife: Can the Blind Ever See? *A.L. Kovacs* • The Research Findings on Gender Issues in Aging Men and Women, *J. Belsky*

Behavioral Science Book Service Selection
1992 224pp 0-8261-7680-1 hardcover

536 Broadway, New York, NY 10012-3955 • (212) 431-4370 • Fax (212) 941-7842

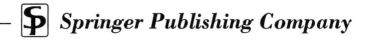
Springer Publishing Company

DILEMMAS IN HUMAN SERVICE MANAGEMENT

Illustrative Case Studies

Raymond Sanchez Mayers, PhD,
Federico Souflee, Jr., PhD,
and **Dick J. Schoech,** PhD

Foreword by Michael J. Austin, PhD.

The authors have combined their experience as teachers and social workers to create actual case studies, with discussion questions to help prepare students for real world problems. A broad range of situations are discussed—from sexual harassment to ethical concerns and management theory.

Contents:

Part I: Human Services Management in Perspective • **Part II : The Case Method** • **Part III: Cases** • An Accounting Clerk for DSS • Status Quo Leadership • Developing an Information System • New Kid on the Block • Breaking Up is Hard To Do • The Rice War • Which Side Are You On? • The Battered Women's Shelter of Aiken County • Planning and the Politics of Inclusion • The Hit Man • Staffing a Planning Committee • The Politically Correct Candidate • Who's the Boss? • New Directions • Whose Values: The Politics of Planning • A Problem Within • A Sexual Harassment Complaint • Inertia on the Board • The Price of Serving • "Creative" Grant Writing for Survival • Too Many Chiefs • Staff Meetings at Senior Citizen Centers of the Valley, Inc.

Springer Series on Social Work
1994 184pp 0-8261-7740-9 hardcover

536 Broadway, New York, NY 10012-3955 • (212) 431-4370 • Fax (212) 941-7842

 **Springer Publishing Company**

THE FAMILY
FUNCTIONING SCALE
*A Guide to Research
and Practice*

Ludwig L. Geismar, PhD, and
Michael Camasso, PhD,
Foreword by **Maxwell Siporin**

A thoroughly current work based on
Dr. Geismar's earlier books about family
functioning. Incorporates the latest modification
of the scale, thus enhancing its clinical utility.

Contents:

Introduction • Standardized Evaluation in Social Welfare
and Related Helping Professions • Measuring the Social
Functioning of Families: Research and Clinical Issues
• Theoretical Underpinnings • Assembling the Family
Functioning Data • Criteria for Evaluating Family Functioning • The Profiling and Rating Process: Guidelines
and an Illustration • Statistical Analysis • Clinical Uses of
the Family Functioning Scale • Past Research and Future
Directions • Appendixes • Bibliography

Springer Series on Social Work
224pp   0-8261-7940-1   hardcover

536 Broadway, New York, NY 10012-3955 • (212) 431-4370 • Fax (212) 941-7842

Springer Publishing Company

WOMEN AND ANGER

Sandra P. Thomas, PhD, RN, Editor

"The study, the first large-scale detailed look at anger in the lives of average middle-class american women, puts the lie to many long-standing beliefs about the role of this emotion in women's lives."
—New York Times

"Thomas and her colleagues make sense out of why anger is a special health problem for women, and why anger is an excellent example of a 'dis-ease' in need of study when considering the evolution of a new health paradigm focusing on the fit between person and environment. It has made me think that how a person handles anger should be a part of every health professional's assessment of a new patient."
—Angela Barron McBride, PhD

Contents:

Emotions and How They Develop, *S. P. Thomas* • Anger and Its Manifestations in Women, *S. P. Thomas* • Anger: Targets and Triggers, *G. Denham and K. Bultemeier* • Women's Anger and Self-Esteem, *M. Saylor and G. Denham* • Stress, Role Responsibilities, Social Support, and Anger, *S.P. Thomas and M. M. Donnellan* • Values and Anger, *C. Smucker, J. Martin, and D. Wilt* • Unhealthy, Unfit, and Too Angry to Care? *M.A. Modrcin-McCarthy and J. Tollett* • Women's Anger and Eating, *S.S. Russell and B. Shirk* • Women's Anger and Substance Use, *E.G. Seabrook* • Women, Depression, and Anger, *P.G. Droppleman and D. Wilt* • Treatment of Anger, *D. Wilt*

Springer Series : Focus on Women
1993 352pp 0-8261-8100-7 hardcover

536 Broadway, New York, NY 10012-3955 • (212) 431-4370 • Fax (212) 941-7842